The Couples Cookbook

Written By: Dennis H. Bunt

Contributor and Taster: Nancy E. Bunt

ISBN-10: 14482541955
ISBN-13: 978-1482541953

<u>Preface</u>

This cookbook was written for partners and couples. All of the recipes in this cookbook are written with ingredients proportioned for two people. We hope you and your partner will enjoy these recipes which are graded as easy, moderate or challenging, with a goal towards simplicity. We've also suggested some beverage pairings with some of the recipes.

If you're allergic or dislike any ingredient, leave it out and substitute something else. Please don't stress about making the dish exactly the same as the recipes in this cookbook. Be creative and make adjustments to the ingredients to suit your tastes. For instance, if you don't like cumin, feel free to substitute a spice or herb that you like and perhaps use oregano or thyme instead.

Also, in many dishes you can leave out the meat or substitute a tofu product and have a wonderful vegetarian dish. You can also substitute the type of meat if you're on a low cholesterol diet in some recipes, try poultry instead of pork as an example.

With regard to the seafood recipes, you can certainly substitute trout for salmon or substitute any firm white fish for cod as an example. Buy the freshest fish in your market and substitute. Ask your fish monger which fish is freshest. Experiment with these recipes, which is one of the great joys of cooking.

Whenever we include olive oil in a recipe we recommend that you use extra virgin olive oil. We like to use sea salt and fresh cracked pepper whenever we season with salt and pepper, it does make a difference. If you use wine in a recipe, use your drinking wine and not a nasty cooking wine from your grocer. We prefer not to use canned goods, such as canned tomatoes or stock when we can find boxed or glass packaging. We also prefer fresh herbs versus dried if we have them.

Taste your food frequently while cooking and adjust your seasoning according. Use fresh vegetables and fruit whenever possible. Please try organic foods and farmer's market produce and avoid products with trans fats, MSG and other unhealthy ingredients. Finally, we like to buy "all natural" and free range meats when we can.

GOOD LUCK !

DEDICATION

This cookbook is dedicated to three women who inspired me to cook and experiment with my cooking. To Gramma Lucia DiPietro, who was the best cook that I ever met. She was born in Sicily and immigrated to America as a young woman in the early 20th century. She created dishes with a wonderful southern Italian flair and could cook any cuisine. I still haven't tasted raviolis, braciole, calamari or meatballs that came close to gram's. To my mother, Raffaela Bunt who showed me many cooking tricks and techniques that I still use today.   And to my lovely wife Nancy who was willing to taste ever dish in this cookbook and many others that didn't make it. They all encouraged me to cook creatively.

This dedication is also to Greg, April and Cooper, we love you guys.

When I started cooking for Nancy many years ago, all of the cookbooks were written with recipes for 4-8 people. That inspired me to create my own recipes for couples and partners, to make it easier to create wonderfully delicious and simple meals using the correct proportion of ingredients, herbs and spices. I also strived for simplicity with just a few ingredients in many recipes. I've been writing my recipes down and this cookbook has been a work in process over the last 8 years or so. Please enjoy and don't fret the small stuff.

Table of Contents

APPETIZERS

Shrimp Wrapped in Bacon
Rating: Easy   Time: 20 minutes

Ingredients:

8 large raw shrimp, shelled and deveined

4 raw slices of your favorite bacon   Tooth picks

Directions:

    Preheat broiler on high (450-500 degrees). Cut each strip of bacon in half and wrap a half strip around each shrimp. Secure the bacon with one toothpick through the bacon and the shrimp. Repeat the process on all of the shrimp. Broil the shrimp (not too close to the burner, the second level may be best depending on your oven). Check the broiling regularly as you don't want to burn the shrimp. Turn the shrimp over once one side is done, meaning the bacon is cooked and the shrimp are pink. Remove from oven when done and cover with aluminum foil to keep warm. It's best if served warm. You can reheat the shrimp under the broiler again for just a few minutes, if you need to.

Bruschetta Tomato Appetizer
Rating: Easy   Time: 10 minutes

Ingredients:

3-4 plum tomatoes, diced   Salt and pepper

2 cloves garlic, crushed   Loaf of French bread

Olive oil

Directions:

    Cut the bread into 10 slices on a bias about ¼ inches thick and lay them on a sheet pan. Toast them under the broiler until they are very lightly toasted on both sides and remove the pan from the oven, leaving the broiler on.

    In a small frying pan sauté the garlic in a little olive oil for 30 seconds on medium heat, being careful not to burn the garlic. Add the tomatoes to the frying pan and a drizzle of olive oil and sauté until the tomatoes are hot and the juice has reduced. Season with salt and pepper to your taste.

Brush the toast (or crostini) with a little olive oil on one side and top it with the sautéed tomatoes. After all crostinis are topped with the tomatoes return the pan to the broiler to toast a little further for a minute or two. Remove the pan, sprinkle the bruschetta with parmesan cheese and serve to your partner with a cold glass of white wine.

Mascarpone Cheese with Nuts and Honey Hors D'oeuvre

Rating: Easy   Time: 20 minutes
Ingredients:
4 oz mascarpone cheese   Crackers – your favorite
½ cup roughly chopped nuts   Honey
Directions:

We like macadamia, almonds or walnuts for this dish. Spread the mascarpone on the crackers and sprinkle the nuts on top. Then drizzle a couple drops of honey on top of the chopped nuts and serve, how easy is that !

Clams Broiled on the Half Shell Hors D'oeuvre

Rating: Moderate   Time: 20 minutes
Ingredients:
24-36 littleneck clams   3 slices, uncooked bacon diced
¼ cup diced green bell pepper   Hot sauce (low / medium heat)
¼ cup diced red bell pepper   Salt
1 tbsp diced shallots or red onion
Directions:

Wash the clam thoroughly with a brush and warm water. Steam the clams in a large pot of salted water until they open. Remove the clams with a slotted spoon to a bowl to cool, (don't overcook the clams as they will get tough). Discard any clams that did not open. Cool them in the refrigerator for 20-30 minutes. Save the clam juice for appetizers or soup in the freezer using a zipper bag. Mix the bacon, peppers and shallots together in a bowl and season with salt. Open one clam and scoop all of the clam meat onto one of the half shells. Repeat with all of the clams. Discard the empty clam shells.

Place each shell on a sheet pan meat side up and pile some of the bacon, pepper and shallot mix on top of the clam meat. Add 1-2 drops of hot sauce to your taste and then repeat again with the second clam and so on. Broil the clams about 2-3 inches from the broiler element until the bacon is sizzling and the peppers start to brown, about 450 degrees. Remove from the oven and serve warm with a cold beer.

English Muffins with Sautéed Onions and Cheese
Rating: Moderate   Time: 30 minutes
Ingredients:
2 large yellow onions   ¼ cup grated parmesan
Olive oil   ¼ cup grated Romano cheese
4 extra large English muffins   ½ tsp red pepper flakes
¼ cup asiago cheese, grated   Salt
Directions:

Skin and cut the onions into quarters and then slice them thin. Sauté the slice onions in 3-4 tbsp of olive oil in a non-stick skillet over medium low heat. Do not brown the onions just sweat them to bring out the sugars and carmelization, reduce the heat accordingly. Season with salt and red pepper flakes. Split and lightly toast the English muffins.

Mix the three cheeses in a bowl. Cut the lightly toasted English muffins into thirds, in the shape of wedges. The onions will take about 7-9 minutes to caramelize; they should taste sweet and tender. Remove them from the skillet and cool for 5 minutes.   Pre-heat the broiler to 450 degrees. Place the muffin wedges on a sheet pan and spoon some onions on top and then top with a little cheese. Broil about 2-3 inches from the broiling element until the cheese starts to melt, watch them carefully.

Remove from the oven and serve warm to your partner with some fruit, veggies and a cold drink.

Pig on a Stick for Two
This is a pork lover's dream appetizer but feel free to use chicken breast meat
Rating: Easy   Time: 20 minutes
Suggested Wines: Red: Cabernet Sauvignon or Pinot Noir, White: Chardonnay
Ingredients:
12-16 oz pork tenderloin   Hot sauce (medium heat)
1 to 2 cups of your favorite spicy/sweet BBQ sauce

10 or 12 wooden skewers soaked in water for 20 minutes

Directions:

Slice the tenderloin lengthwise into long thin strips (about 1 inch thick). Marinate the pork in 1 cup of barbecue sauce while the grill is heating up.

Preheat the gas grill (20 minutes) or charcoal grill (until the coals are red hot). If you prefer you can broil the pork in the oven, set the broiler to high and put the rack on the second level from the top. Slide the pork strips onto the wooden skewers. Grill 3-5 minutes each side depending on how hot your grill or broiler gets and the thickness of the meat, the pork should be charred on the outside and a little pink inside. Brush on more barbecue sauce once when you turn the skewers and once when you take them off the grill or out of the oven. Use a thermometer if you're uncertain if the pork is done or not. Serve the pork right on the skewers to your loved one or make a meal out of it and serve with garlic smashed potatoes and cooked peas.

Sausage and Sour Cream Dip

Rating: Easy   Time: 20 minutes

Ingredients:

4-6 oz pork smoked sausage (loose and not in casings)

6-8 oz sour cream   Bagel chips or crackers

3 scallions, chopped   Salt and pepper

½ cup red bell pepper, diced

Directions:

Fry the sausage in vegetable or olive oil until cooked, breaking the meat apart with a spatula as it cooks. Drain the grease from the pan and let sausage cool. Add the cooked sausage, sour cream, bell pepper and scallions to a bowl and mix well. Season with salt and pepper to your taste. Serve with chips, crackers or tortilla sections for dipping. This dip can be served either warm or cold. We prefer it warm. To spice it up a bit add a tsp of diced jalapeno pepper.

Shrimp and Horseradish Appetizer

This would also make an excellent main course

Rating: Easy   Time: 20 minutes

Ingredients:

18 – 20 large cooked shrimp, shelled and deveined

½ cup sour cream

1 tbsp mayonnaise

1 tbsp prepared horseradish

3-4 scallions, chopped

Salt and pepper

Party toothpicks or crackers

Directions:

Add the sour cream, mayonnaise, horseradish and scallions to a bowl and mix well. Taste and season with salt and pepper to your liking. Add more horseradish if you like it a little spicy. Fold in the shrimp and mix well. Spoon the shrimp onto a serving dish and accompany with party toothpicks or spoon onto high quality crackers.

Steak with Roasted Red Peppers

Rating: Moderate
Time: 30 minutes

Ingredients:

1 small steak (sirloin or strip)

1 bottle horseradish spread

Olive oil

1 jar Italian roasted whole red peppers

Salt and pepper

Dry rub (your favorite brand)

Toothpicks

Directions:

Cut the steak into small cubes, no more than 1 inch square. Season the cut steak with dry rub and salt and pepper. On medium heat fry the steak in a skillet in 1-2 tbsp of olive oil until done (just a couple of minutes – stirring a couple of times to brown evenly but a little red inside). Remove the steak to a plate to cool. Cut the roasted red peppers into thin strips, about 2-3 inches long (or long enough to wrap around one of your steak cubes) and 1 inch wide. After the steak has cooled, wrap each piece of steak with a strip of roasted red pepper and secure with a toothpick. Lay all the wrapped steak cubes on serving plate and squirt a dab of horseradish spread on top and re-season with salt and pepper and serve warm.

Bruschetta Tapenade Appetizer

Rating: Easy
Time: 10 minutes

Ingredients:

20 green olives with pimento

Olive oil

Salt and pepper

20 black pitted kalamata olives

Loaf of French bread

Directions:

Place the olives in a food processor or mini-processor, drizzle in 1 tbsp of olive oil and pulse until the olives are roughly chopped. Taste the tapenade and add pepper or salt to your liking. If the mix is a little too thick add a little more olive oil and pulse a few more times. You want the olive tapenade to be course and not a puree.

Cut the bread into slices on a bias about 1/2 inch thick. Toast them under the broiler until they are very lightly toasted on both sides and remove them from oven, leaving broiler on. Spoon the tapenade on the toast and return to the broiler to toast a little further. Remove, sprinkle with parmesan cheese and serve to your partner with some crisp cold white wine or champagne.

Chicken Wing Hors D'oeuvres Healthy Style

Rating: Moderate   <u>Time</u>: 60-75 minutes

Notes: This could be a whole meal or football game snack for the two of you

Ingredients:

1 dozen fresh chicken wings	Vegetable oil for greasing the pan
1 bottle spicy barbeque sauce	1 cup ranch/blue cheese dressing
1 tbsp hot sauce	2 celery stalks cut into 4 in. pieces
Salt and pepper	

Directions:

Chicken wings have three sections, with two joints. Break or loosen the joints with your fingers by bending them back and forth. Cut through the two joints with a sharp knife to separate each wing into 3 sections, the meaty "drumstick", the middle wing and the wing tip. The wing tip has very little meat and is best reserved for making chicken broth so don't use them in this recipe. You should have 24 pieces of chicken remaining. Boil these pieces in a stock pot of water, seasoned with salt and pepper for 20 minutes. Remove the chicken to a mixing bowl lined with paper towels in the bottom and dry the chicken with paper towels once they have cooled. Pre-heat the oven to 375 degrees. Remove the wet paper towels from the bowl and pour one cup of barbeque sauce and the hot sauce on top of the chicken. Season with salt and pepper. Stir the chicken with a long spoon to spread the sauce evenly over the chicken pieces. Add more barbeque sauce if the chicken is not fully coated. With tongs arrange the chicken on a greased flat baking pan and bake for 25 minutes. Remove the chicken and serve hot with blue cheese or ranch dressing and celery.

Crab and Spinach Dip

Rating: Moderate   Time: 20 minutes

Ingredients:

4 oz crab meat (pre-cooked)   1 tbsp sour cream

1 tbsp red bell pepper, diced   Salt and pepper

1 handful fresh spinach, chopped   1-2 tbsp breadcrumbs

1 tbsp mayonnaise

2-3 tortillas, fajita size (each fajita cut into six wedges)

1 tbsp shredded cheese (cheddar or pepper jack)

Optional: ½ Jalapeno pepper, finely diced

Directions:

Mix all of the ingredients, except the breadcrumbs and tortillas, in a bowl and season with salt and pepper to taste (add the jalapeno now if you wish). Pre-heat the oven to 400 degrees. Pour the dip into a small casserole dish. Sprinkle the breadcrumbs on top. Bake on the middle rack for 10-15 minutes or until the dip is hot, but not bubbling. Remove the dip to cool a little before serving. Place the tortilla wedges on a plate and heat in your microwave oven for about 30 seconds, or until warm, but not hot, this softens the tortillas. Serve the dip with the wedges for dipping. Enjoy.

Escargot with Cream and Biscuits

Suggested wines: chilled whites such as chardonnay, pinot grigio, sauvignon blanc or a light merlot

Ratings: Moderate   Time: 20 minutes

Ingredients:

1 small can medium cooked snails, drained

2 large frozen biscuits from your grocer (your favorite brand)

1 cup of half and half   1 shallot/onion chopped fine

1 tsp of dried or fresh tarragon   2 tbsp of olive oil

Salt and pepper to taste   2 tbsp of butter

Directions:

Bake the biscuits in an oven according to the package directions (keep warm if the biscuits are baked before the snails are cooked). In a small skillet brown the shallots in the olive oil over medium low heat for 3-4 minutes being careful not to brown the shallots. Add the snails and heat for 1-2 minutes. Add the cream, tarragon and salt and pepper and simmer to reduce by 50%. Taste the sauce and re-season if needed. Add the butter last and stir the sauce until it's all melted and incorporated. Cut each biscuit in half so that you have one top and on bottom for each. Place the bottom biscuit half on a small plate or bowl. Pour half of the snails and cream mixture on the bottom biscuit. Place the top of the biscuit on top of the snails. Repeat the process for other serving.

Lobster, Shrimp and Cheese on Toast
Rating: Moderate   Time: 20 minutes
Ingredients:
½ lb lobster meat, chopped   ¼ tsp pepper
12 small cooked, shelled shrimp   ½ tsp salt
1 cup grated mozzarella   1 loaf French bread
Directions:
    Slice the bread into medium thick slices (about ½ inch). Arrange the slices on a cookie sheet and toast lightly in the oven on both sides under the broiler. Remove the bread from the oven. Mix the other ingredients in a bowl and spoon onto the toasted bread and place it under the broiler until the cheese is melted. Serve warm.

Mussels Steamed in Wine with Garlic
Rating: Moderate   Time: 20 minutes
Suggested Wines: Dry white wines such as chardonnay or pinot grigio
Bread: Fresh Italian or French crusty bread is a must with this dish to soak up the wine sauce
Ingredients:
2-3 dozen fresh mussels (thoroughly cleaned with the beards removed)
1 cup dry white wine (one that you would drink)
4 cloves crushed garlic   2-3 tbsp olive oil
1 small onion finely diced   ½ cup chopped scallions
Salt and pepper to taste   Optional: ¼ tsp red pepper flakes
Directions:
    In a large stock pot heat the olive oil and sauté the onions on medium low

heat being careful not to brown the onions. After 4-5 minutes reduce the heat to low add the garlic and sauté for about a minute to extract the aroma, do not brown the garlic (remove the pan from the burner if the garlic starts to brown). Add the wine, increase the heat to medium and bring the wine to a simmer. Add the mussels, salt, pepper and cover the pan. Simmer for 4-5 minutes until the mussels open up. Discard any mussels than don't open.   Taste the sauce and re-season as you desire.   Spoon the mussels and the wonderfully flavorful sauce into two bowls and sprinkle with scallions. Serve with slices of crusty bread.

Prosciutto and Asparagus Appetizer

Rating: Easy   Time: 10 minutes

Ingredients:

12-14 spears of fresh asparagus   Salt and pepper to taste

6-8 slices of prosciutto, sliced thin

Directions:

        In a medium frying pan add 2 cups of well salted water and bring it to a slow simmer. Cut the bottoms off the asparagus by breaking the ends off with your hands. The asparagus will break at the point the tough portion of the root connects with the tender shoot. Place them into the boiling water for about 2-3 minutes, or until the asparagus is tender (taste a piece for tenderness to your liking). Remove them and cool them down by rinsing them in a colander under cold water for several minutes or by submerging in an ice water bath. Dry the asparagus on paper towel. Cut the prosciutto into thin strips and wrap the strips around the asparagus spears in a spiral from top to bottom. Arrange them on a large plate and serve.

Scallop and Shrimp Kabobs

Rating: Moderate   Time: 45 minutes

Suggested Wines: Dry or semi-dry white wines such as pinot grigio

Ingredients:

6 large scallops   Butter

6 large shelled shrimp   Salt and pepper

6 cherry tomatoes   6 skewers

Commercial seafood seasoning   6 medium mushrooms

2 medium yellow onions (skinned and cut into quarters)

1 red bell pepper cut into squares, (approx. 2 inches x 2 inches)
Directions:

Soak wooden skewers for 30 minutes in water before cooking. On each skewer arrange the scallops, shrimp, onion quarters, bell pepper and mushrooms alternating between the shellfish and the vegetable, making sure that you have one scallop and one shrimp on each skewer. Don't add the cherry tomatoes yet.

Season the kabobs with salt, pepper and your favorite seafood seasoning. Grill on a preheated grill on one side for 2-3 minutes or until the shellfish cooks and vegetables start to brown. Turn the skewers half a turn and grill 2-3 minutes and then turn another half turn and brown 2-3 minutes. The shrimp will be done when they turn pink and the scallops will be done when they turn white and are no longer translucent. The shrimp and scallops will take about the same time to cook. During the last 2 minutes of grilling add the cherry tomatoes to the skewers and brown a little. Serve alone or to make a meal over cooked rice.

Meatballs Southwest Style
Rating: Challenging   Time: 60 minutes
Suggested Beverage: A cold micro brew beer or a cold white wine such as pinot grigio or sauvignon blanc
Suggested Sides: Guacamole salad and tortilla chips
Ingredients:
Meatballs:

¼ lb ground veal (or beef)	½ tsp cayenne pepper
¼ lb ground pork (or turkey)	½ tsp ground cumin
1 egg	½ tsp chili powder
1 tbsp seasoned breadcrumbs	½ tsp salt

Sauce:

25-30 oz diced tomatoes	½ medium yellow onion diced
1 tsp ground cumin	½ cup chopped fresh cilantro
1 tsp chili powder	½ tsp salt
1 small jalapeno, diced	

Topping: ½ cup shredded Monterey Jack cheese (or cheddar)
Directions:

Mix all of the ingredients for the sauce in a mixing bowl, stir to combine and allow to rest for the flavors to merge for 30 minutes. Taste and re-season. Note that the sauce will get hotter as the jalapeno seeds flavor the sauce so be careful about adding more heat at this time.

In a mixing bowl combine all of the ingredients for the spicy meatballs with your hands and form small meatballs, about the 1-1/2 inches in diameter (smaller than a golf ball). Heat a medium non-stick skillet on medium heat with 2 tbsp of olive oil. Transfer the meatballs one at a time into the hot oil. Roll them over when they brown on one side trying to brown them all around. They should have a nice charred crust. Add more oil as needed. When they are browned on all sides add the sauce to the skillet and scrape the bottom of the pan to release the meat bits. Stir and cook for 4-5 minutes so that the sauce simmers lightly and serve on dinner plates with toothpicks and sprinkle with cheese and with tortilla chips.

Steak Skewers Appetizer

Rating: Moderate   Time: 2 hours
Notes: You can also make this appetizer with lamb for a little variety
Ingredients:

1lb sirloin or strip steak	1 tsp hot sauce
½ cup soy sauce, plus 3 tbsp	Sesame seeds
Juice from 1 fresh lime	Olive oil

Directions:

Combine ½ cup soy sauce, lime juice, hot sauce and 1 cup of water in a zipper bag for the marinade. Cut the steak or lamb into thin strips of meat about 5-7 inches long. Toss the meat strips into the zip bag and close the bag tight.

Shake the bag so that the meat and marinade are well distributed. Refrigerate for 90 minutes to overnight. Soak wooden skewers for 30 minutes in water before grilling. Heat a grill pan (with a little olive oil) on the stove or use an outdoor grill. Remove the meat to a plate and save some of the marinade for brushing on the meat during grilling. Discard the rest. Slide the meat strips on the skewers. Grill the meat on one side until it's charred and then flip and grill the other side. Brush the meat a couple of times with the saved marinade. When the meat is charred on 2 sides it should be done, about 3 minutes a side depending on how hot your grill is. The center of the meat should still be a little red for medium rare. Remove the skewers to a plate and sprinkle sesame seeds on top. Create a little dipping sauce by mixing 3 tbsp of soy sauce with 6 tbsp of water, a pinch of sesame seeds and a couple of dashes of hot sauce, stirred well. Do not use the marinade for dipping, discard it. Enjoy.

Steak Crostini
Rating: Easy   Time: 10 minutes
Ingredients:
4-6 slices sandwich steak   2 tbsp mayonnaise
2 cloves garlic, crushed   1 tsp prepared horseradish
Olive oil   Loaf of French bread
Salt and pepper
Directions:
    Cut the bread into slices on a bias about 1/2 inch thick, about 10 slices. Toast them under the broiler until they are very lightly toasted on both sides and remove them from oven, leaving the broiler on.   Mix the mayonnaise and horseradish in a bowl. In a small frying pan fry the steak in 1 tbsp of olive oil on medium heat until brown on both sides and reduce the heat and add the garlic for about 30 seconds. Season with salt and pepper to your taste. Remove the steak from the pan and cut into pieces that are about the same size as the bread slices. Brush the toast (or crostini) with a little olive oil on one side and top with the steak. Return to the broiler to toast a little further. Remove the pan from the oven and top each piece of steak with a little of the mayo mix and serve.

Clam and Artichoke Dip
Rating: Easy   Time: 40 minutes
Ingredients:
Dip:
1 can of clams retain the juice, about 14 oz
1 jar chopped artichokes drained, about 14 oz
2 – 3 scallions, chopped   ½ tsp salt
8 oz sour cream   ¼ tsp pepper
½ cup mayonnaise
Other: Crackers for dipping or toasted French bread slices
Directions:
    Mix all the ingredients for the dip in a mixing bowl well. Taste and re-season with salt and pepper. Pre-heat the oven to 350 degrees. Pour the dip

ingredients into a casserole dish and bake on a middle rack, uncovered for 25-30 minutes, or until the dip is bubbling and has thickened. Remove the dish, stir the dip and allow to cool uncovered, this will help to thicken the dip. Serve with crackers either at room temperature or warm.

Escargot with White Wine
This is an elegant and romantic appetizer
Rating: Easy   Time: 10 minutes
Suggested Wines: Chardonnay or pinto grigio for this opening course
Ingredients:
1 small can escargot, drained   Olive oil
4 tbsp red bell pepper, diced   Salt and pepper to taste
½ cup dry white wine   2 slices fresh Italian bread
4 clove garlic, chopped
Directions:
Sauté the bell pepper in a pan with olive oil over medium low heat for 2 minutes. Add the garlic and cook for one minute, remove pan from heat if garlic starts to brown. Add the white wine, the snails, salt and pepper and simmer at medium heat for 2-3 minutes, until the wine is reduced by 50%. While the snails are cooking, toast the bread and cut into toast points for dipping. Divide the snails and wine sauce into equal parts in two small bowls or ramekins.

Mango Salsa Appetizer, Snack or Topping
This sweet and spicy salsa is a unique blend of flavors that will wow your partner
Rating: Easy   Time: 15 minutes
Suggestions: Serve the salsa with tortilla chips as a pre-dinner snack or spoon on top of salmon or chicken before baking in the oven as an entree.
Ingredients:
1 ripe and soft mango   1 tsp ground cumin
1 tbsp jalapeno pepper, diced   1 tsp of fresh cilantro or dried
1 tbsp red or yellow onion, diced   ½ tsp salt
Optional: the juice from a fresh lime, don't use bottled lime juice
Directions:
The center of a mango has a pit that is long and somewhat flat. Peel the mango and the cut slices away from the pit. Use a paper towel to hold the

mango while peeling with either a paring knife or a peeler as the mango is very slippery when peeled. The fruit next to the pit is somewhat tough and should be trimmed off your slices and discarded. Then dice the mango into ½ inch pieces. Transfer the diced mango to a mixing bowl and add all the other ingredients and stir. Taste the salsa and add more cumin or salt to your taste. Let the salsa sit in the refrigerator (covered) for an hour or so and taste for re-seasoning.

Chocolate and Peanut Butter Hors D'oeuvres
This is a great date night appetizer when served with cold sparkling wine, like Prosecco

Rating: Moderate   Time: 20 minutes
Ingredients:
4 oz mini chocolate chips   12-18 fresh raspberries
4 tbsp chunky peanut butter   1 loaf French bread
Directions:

Slice 10-15 slices of bread off of the French loaf, about ½ inch thick. Toast the slices lightly under the broiler on both sides. Let the toast cool. Spread a layer of peanut butter on top and then top with a small mound of chocolate chips. Broil them about 2-3 inches from the broiler element, set at 450 degrees, until the chocolate and peanut butter melts a little. You should watch them carefully to avoid having a melted mess. Remove the hors d'oeuvres from the oven and top each one with a fresh raspberry and serve your partner with a semi sweet sparkling wine. Use baking paper to reduce the clean-up to your baking pan.

Beef Puff Pastry Pot Pie (or venison, turkey)
Rating: Moderate   Time: 30 minutes
Ingredients:
½ lb ground meat, your choice   3 scallions chopped
1 tsp ground cumin   ⅓ cup bell pepper, chopped
1 tsp chili powder   Olive oil
1 tsp garlic powder   Salt and pepper to taste
½ tsp cayenne pepper or to taste   ⅓ cup cheddar cheese, shredded

Parchment paper   Non-stick cooking spray
1 roll of puff pastry, rolled thin with a rolling pin
Directions:

    Fry the meat in 1-2 tbsp of olive oil in a medium non-stick skillet on medium heat. Drain the excess grease from the pan when the meat is nearly finished cooking. Add all of the spices and herbs to the meat and stir. Remove the meat from the pan and cool in a bowl. Add the scallions and pepper to the same skillet and sauté on medium low heat for 3-4 minutes or until soft. Pour the cooked veggies in with the meat and cool in the refrigerator. Pre-heat the oven to 375 degrees. Drain some of the juices out of the ground meat bowl if any accumulated in the bowl as it cooled. Using a round cookie cutter or a large drinking glass cut rounds in the puff pastry dough (about 3-4 inches in diameter), as many as you can get out of one sheet of dough.

    Spray a cookie sheet with non-stick cooking spray. Lay a sheet of parchment paper on the sprayed cookie sheet and then spray the top of the parchment paper. Lay the dough rounds on the parchment paper and then spoon the ground beef mixture in the middle, do not overload the dough. Sprinkle on some cheese and then fold over the dough to make a half moon. With a fork crimp down the edges of the dough. It helps to rinse your fork with water to get it wet for crimping. Repeat with each dough round. Bake the stuffed hors d'oeuvre for 20-25 minutes or until the dough is golden brown. Serve warm to your partner with a cold drink.

Shellfish Crostini

Rating: Moderate   Time: 30 minutes
Suggested Wines: A sweet or semi sweet wine such as riesling or sauvignon blanc
Ingredients:
12 medium raw bay scallops, washed
12 medium raw shrimp, shelled and deveined
1 loaf French bread   ½ medium yellow onion, chopped
Olive oil   Salt and pepper to taste
3 tbsp bell pepper, chopped   ½ cup shredded provolone cheese
3 tbsp seasoned breadcrumbs

Directions:

Sauté the shrimp, scallops, onions and bell pepper in a hot medium frying pan with 2 tbsp of olive oil on medium heat for a couple of minutes until the shrimp are pink and the scallops are no longer translucent, stirring frequently. Let them cool and pour into a mini food processor or a blender. Add salt, pepper, bread crumbs and drizzle in 1 tbsp of olive oil and pulse a few times until the shrimp and scallops are chopped rough, but not pureed. Slice the bread on a bias about 1/2 inch thick, making 10-12 slices. Toast under the broiler on a cookie sheet until lightly toasted on each side. Remove from the oven and leave the broiler on. Brush the toast or crostini with olive oil on one side and top with a heaping tbsp (or more) of the chopped shellfish mixture. Sprinkle each crostini with a little cheese and broil 2 inches from the broiler element until the cheese melts. Remove to a serving plate and serve with some cold semi-sweet or sweet white wine.

Spinach and Artichoke Dip Appetizer or Lunch
This is a delicious appetizer before dinner or for lunch

Rated: Easy   Time: 20 Minutes

Dip:

One frozen package (12 oz.) chopped spinach, thawed

1 cup of chopped canned artichokes, drained

2 tbsp of mayonnaise

1 cup of grated sharp cheddar cheese

1 jalapeno pepper, chopped (optional)

Salt and pepper to taste

Topping:

3-4 tbsp of grated parmesan cheese (optional)

Chips:

1 bag of your favorite tortilla chips (12-16 oz)

Directions:

Squeeze the thawed spinach between sheets of paper towel to remove the water. Mix all of the dip ingredients into a large mixing bowls. Stir to combine. Taste the dip for salt and pepper seasoning. Preheat oven to 375 degrees. Pour the dip into a casserole dish. Place the casserole dish on a sheet pan in case the dip bubbles over. Bake in oven for 15 to 20 minutes uncovered or until the mixture is bubbling hot. Remove from oven and sprinkle with a little grated parmesan cheese and serve with the tortilla chips. This dip is best serve warm.

Italian Style Stuffed Mushrooms

Rating: Moderate   Time: 30 minutes

Ingredients:

12 large stuffing mushrooms, rinsed and stems removed

3-4 pieces sun-dried tomatoes   Salt and pepper

½ medium yellow onion, diced   Olive oil

1 large clove garlic, cut in quarters   ¾ cup season breadcrumbs

¼ tsp dried basil   Parmesan cheese

Directions:

If your sun dried tomatoes are hard, you will need so soften them by immersing them in a cup of boiling water for 2-3 minutes. In a mini microprocessor or a blender add the mushroom stems, salt, pepper, basil, sundried tomatoes, garlic, onion and breadcrumbs and chop until fine. Then drizzle in 1 tbsp of olive oil and 1 tbsp of water and pulse to combine. The stuffing should be a little bit moist – so add a little more water and olive oil to moisten. Taste the stuffing and re-season. Pre-heat the oven to 350 degrees and brush the bottom of a baking pan with oil, just large enough to hold all the mushrooms. Stuff each mushroom cap with the stuffing, until it mounds on top. Place in the pan stuffing side up. Bake for 15 minutes or until the mushroom caps are tender. Remove the pan from the oven and turn on the broiler. Sprinkle a fair amount of parmesan cheese on each mushroom and broil 2-3 inches from the broiler element, until the cheese is charred. Remove and serve with a cold martini or a sweet cocktail.

Seafood Entrées

Salmon or Steelhead Trout with Mango Salsa

Rating: Moderate   Time: 30 minutes

Suggested Wine: White: pinot grigio or chardonnay. Red: a light merlot.

Ingredients:

1 lb salmon filet cut into two pieces, skin removed

1 ripe / soft mango   2 tbsp olive oil

½ cup chopped bell pepper   1 tbsp parsley, chopped

Salt and pepper for seasoning

Optional: 1 tbsp of chopped jalapeno pepper

Directions:

We prefer a thick piece of salmon and not a thin tail portion. Always rinse and dry your fish with paper towels. Preheat oven to 350 degrees. Brush oil on the salmon top and bottom and place the filets in a roasting pan (glass pans work well with fish). Peal the mango and with a sharp knife or peeler and cut the fruit off of the pit and discard any tough pieces. Chop mango into ½ inch pieces. (Hint: if the mango is not fully ripened you can cook the mango for 5 minutes in a half cup of water in a sauce pan and with a teaspoon of sugar to soften and sweeten the fruit). Combine the mango and peppers in a bowl and spoon onto the salmon filets. Season the top of the salmon with salt and pepper. Bake salmon for 20 minutes or until done.

Salmon Topped with Mascarpone Cheese

The sweetness of the mascarpone complements the salmon taste

Rating: Easy   Time: 30 minutes

Ingredients:

1 lb skinned salmon fillet cut in half   4 tbsp unflavored mascarpone

1 tbsp olive oil   1 tbsp chopped parsley

Salt and pepper

Optional: 6 cooked large shrimp, shell removed

Directions:

Pre-heat oven to 350 degrees. Rinse and dry the fish and rub a little olive oil on all sides of the fish. Season with salt and pepper and place in a roasting pan. Roast for 20 minutes in the oven. Open the oven door and spoon the mascarpone cheese on each fillet. Close the oven and watch the cheese melt (just a couple of minutes).   If you wish to add shrimp to the dish, place the cooked shrimp on top of the mascarpone. Remove the salmon from the oven once the cheese has started to melt and transfer to dinner plates, spooning the cheese over the fish. Sprinkle with a little parsley.

Salmon Savory Cheese Cake

A very interesting main course dish or appetizer. This is not a dessert.

Rating: Moderate   Time: 30 minutes

Suggested Wines: Semi dry white wines such as sauvignon blanc

Ingredients:

8-10 oz salmon filet, skinned   Sour cream

¼ cup dry white wine   2 eggs

Bay leaf   1 medium jalapenos, diced finely

Salt and pepper   1 sleeve of Ritz™ crackers

8 oz cream cheese   1 scallion, chopped

Directions:

Crush the crackers in a zip lock bag. Poach (slow simmer) the salmon in 1 inch of water with the white wine and bay leaf for 20 minutes until cooked through in a skillet on medium heat, season with salt and pepper.   Remove the salmon to a mixing bowl and cool. Preheat the oven to 350 degrees. Once the salmon cools add the cream cheese and eggs and mix well with an electric mixer. Add the jalapenos, ½ cup sour cream, ½ tsp salt and pepper and mix another minute.

Spray a small spring form pan with non-stick cooking spray and pour the crackers in the bottom. Press the crackers tight to the pan. Pour the cream cheese and salmon mix into the spring form pan. Bake for 30-40 minutes. Test to see if it's done with a toothpick. Stick the toothpick in the cake and if it comes out clean it's done. Serve the savory cheese cake warm with a dollop of sour cream and some scallions on top.

Salmon Topped with Crab Meat
The crab meat and salmon pare very well together
Rating: Easy   Time: 30 minutes
Suggested Wines: Dry white wines such as pinot grigio
Ingredients:

1 lb skinned salmon filet	6-8 oz cooked crab meat
1-2 tbsp olive oil	Salt and pepper

1 cup chopped nuts such as walnuts or almonds (optional)
Directions:

Cut the fish in half. Brush olive oil on both sides of the salmon and place the salmon in a glass casserole dish or roasting pan. Salt and pepper the fish. Preheat the oven to 350 degrees. Pat the salmon with the chopped nuts on all sides. Season the crab meat with salt and pepper and then top the salmon with the crab meat. Bake for 20 minutes. Remove to dinner plates and serve.

Salmon Encrusted with Pecans
This dish has a wow factor, impress your partner
Rating: Easy   Time: 30 minutes
Suggested Wines: Chilled chardonnay or pinto grigio
Ingredients:

1 cup chopped pecans	1-2 tbsp olive oil
1 lb skinned salmon filet	

Directions:

Preheat the oven to 350. Cut the fish in half and brush the salmon fillets on both sides with oil. Chop the nuts, the best way to chop pecans is in a mini food processor with pulsating chopping. Do not chop too fine, the pecan pieces should be about the size of raw rice or larger. Lay the salmon fillets in a lightly oil baking dish. Pat the chopped pecans around the salmon with your hands. Bake in a preheated oven for 20 minutes.

Mahi-mahi or Salmon, Baked with a Peach & Jalapeno Topping

The sweetness of the peaches combined with the succulent fish flavors make for a rich tasting dish

Rating: Easy   Time: 30 minutes

Suggested Wine: A dry white wine such as pinto grigio or white Bordeaux

Ingredients:

1 lb skinned fish filet cut in half	3 scallions, chopped
2 ripe peaches, or canned	¼ tsp ground cumin
½ cup red bell pepper, diced	Salt
½ jalapeno finely diced	Olive oil

Directions:

Preheat oven to 350 degrees. Oil the filets on both sides with a little olive oil and place them in a small baking dish and season with a little salt.   Peel the peaches and dice into ½ inch cubes. If you're using canned or bottled peaches measure about 1 cup of peach slices and them chop roughly, do not add any syrup to the mixing bowl.   Combine the peaches, bell pepper, jalapeno and scallions in a mixing bowl with ½ tsp of salt and cumin. Pile the peach salsa on top of each filet and bake on a middle rack for 20 minutes. Remove from the oven and serve hot.

Salmon Grilled with Nuts and Vegetables

Rating: Moderate   Time: 40 minutes

Suggested Wines: A light semi-dry white such as soave or chenin blanc

Ingredients:

1 lb salmon filet, skin on	½ bell pepper cut into thick strips
1 medium zucchini	Salt and pepper
1 medium yellow squash	½ cup pecans or walnuts
2 medium carrots	Olive oil

Directions:

Preheat your charcoal or gas grill for about 20 minutes and clean the grill well. Cut the filet in half and leave skin on. Chop the nuts in a mini food processor or blender until roughly chopped, chop in pulses so that the pieces are not too small. Brush a little olive oil on top of each filet, season with salt and pepper and mound the pecans on top, and press down lightly to help the nuts to stick to the filets. Peel the carrots and cut them in half, lengthwise. Cut the zucchini and squash in quarters lengthwise also.

Lightly brush a little olive oil on all the veggies and season with salt and pepper. When the grill is hot, place the salmon on the grill, skin side down (and do not flip the salmon at all during the grilling). Reduce the heat to medium high. Also, place the carrots on the grill, as the carrots take a little longer to cook than the other veggies. After 5 minutes place the squash, zucchini and peppers on the grill. Turn the vegetables as soon as you have grill marks on one side. Remove the vegetables from the grill after they have been charred a little on both sides to a plate and cover. Once the vegetables have been removed close the cover of the grill and lower the heat to medium. Remove the salmon filets after about 20 minutes of total grilling time, the edges of the salmon should be a little charred and the top firmed up. The skin can be easy removed after grilling.

Salmon Cakes with Melted Mozzarella

This is a succulent dinner recipe that will impress your partner
Rating: Challenging   Time: 30 minutes
Suggested Wines: Dry or semi dry white wines such as white Bordeaux
Ingredients:

12 oz fresh salmon, skin removed	½ red bell pepper, diced
¼ cup seasoned breadcrumbs	3 scallions, chopped
1 tbsp prepared horseradish	1 tsp yellow or spicy mustard
¼ tsp dried thyme	Thousand Island dressing
Juice from ½ lemon	Olive oil
1 tsp salt and ½ tsp pepper	4 slices mozzarella cheese

Directions:

Poach the salmon as follows.   In a large non-stick skillet add 1-2 inches of water and the lemon juice and season with salt and pepper. Heat the water until it's simmering and add the salmon. The water should come to the top of the salmon or just cover it. Simmer for 15 minutes or until the salmon is cooked through and no longer pink inside. Remove the salmon to a paper towel covered plate to dry. Drain and dry the skillet to be used for frying the salmon cakes.

Once the salmon has cooled, transfer it to a mixing bowl and break it up into little pieces with a fork or potato masher. Add the horseradish, peppers, scallions, thyme, breadcrumbs, mustard, salt and pepper to the bowl and mix well with your hands. You may need to add more breadcrumbs to help bind the meat together. Taste and re-season. Divide the salmon mix into 4 separate patties and place in the freezer for 10-15 minutes to set up, on a plate covered with wax or baking paper. Heat the pan with 3 tbsp of olive oil. Brown the salmon cakes in the skillet, until a crust forms on one side and flip and brown them pretty well on the other side also. When they are grilled on both sides place a slice of cheese on top and reduce the heat and cover the pan long enough to melt the cheese. Serve warm to your partner with a dollop of Thousand Island dressing.

Salmon and Avocado With Shrimp
Not only delicious but it's also healthy

Rating: Easy   Time: 45 minutes
Suggested Wines: Whites such as chardonnay and sauvignon blanc and some lighter reds such as merlot
Ingredients:

1 lb skinned salmon filet	¼ cup of diced red bell pepper
1 ripe avocado, skinned & diced	¼ cup diced onion
1 tbsp of mayonnaise	Olive oil
1 pinch of red pepper flakes	Optional: 6 cooked large shrimp
Salt and pepper to taste	

Directions:

Cut the fish in half. Preheat the oven to 350 degrees. In a mixing bowl add the avocado, mayonnaise, bell pepper and onion. Smash the mix roughly with a fork or potato masher. Season with salt and pepper to taste. Add the red pepper flakes if you desire a little heat. Lightly oil each filet and place them on a lightly oiled baking dish. Season the top of each filet with salt and pepper. Bake for 20 minutes and then spoon the avocado mix evenly over each filet. Don't worry if a little avocado over flows over the sides of the fish. Also, add the shrimp at this time. Bake for 3-4 minutes more and serve.

Cod or Scrod Baked with Onions and Tomatoes
Rating: Moderate   Time: 30 minutes
Suggested Wine: Chilled pinot grigio or chardonnay.

Ingredients:

1 lb cod or scrod filet, skinned

1 ripe tomato, sliced thin

1 med. onion, halved & sliced thin

1 tsp capers

½ cup milk

Salt and pepper

4 tbsp of olive oil

1 tbsp of parsley, chopped

1 cup seasoned breadcrumbs

Directions:

Cut filet in half. Add the milk and breadcrumbs into separate bowls or plates. Preheat a large non stick and oven safe skillet on medium on the stove and also preheat the oven to 350.   Sauté the onions in 2 tbsp olive oil for 4-5 minutes until slightly brown. Remove the onions from the skillet to a small bowl and add the rest of the oil to the skillet. Dip the cod filets in the milk and then dip it into the bread crumbs and place in the skillet and brown on one side (about 2 minutes), flip and brown the other side, adding more oil if the fish absorbs the oil. Turn off the heat and place the cooked onions, then the tomatoes and capers on top of the cod. Then move the skillet to the oven to finish the cooking, for about 10-12 minutes or until cooked through and not translucent. Sprinkle with parsley and serve your partner.

Cod or Haddock with Shrimp and a Bacon Crust

Rating: Moderate   Time: 30 minutes

Suggested Wine: Chilled sauvignon blanc or chardonnay.

Ingredients:

1 lb skinned cod or haddock

10 med. shrimp, shelled/deveined

4 strips diced bacon

1 cup bread crumbs

1 cup diced sweet onion

3 tbsp olive oil

2-3 cloves garlic, crushed

½ cup fresh parsley

3 tbsp butter   3 tbsp diced tomatoes

Salt and pepper

Directions for crust:

Crisp bacon in a small frying pan in 1 tbsp of oil on medium heat. Add onions to pan once the bacon is crisp and cook for 5 minutes more on low, being careful not to brown the onions. Add the garlic for 1 minute, being careful not to burn the garlic. Remove cooked ingredients from the burner and pour into a mixing bowl. Combine bread crumbs, parsley and cooked ingredients, cool for a minute or two and season with fresh cracked pepper.

Directions for fish and shrimp:

Preheat oven to 350 degrees. Cut the fish into 2 pieces. Lightly oil a baking dish and add the fish, season fish with a little salt. Coat the top of the fish with the bacon crust mixture. Do not pile on too thick, the crust coating should be light. Bake for 10 minutes and add the shrimp and bake another 10 minutes or until done, fish should be white inside and not translucent, and the shrimp should be pink. Remove the dish from the oven and transfer fish and shrimp with a spatula to individual dinner plates or to a serving plate and spoon on 2 or 3 tbsp of diced tomatoes on top of each fish fillet and season with salt and pepper.

Haddock, Cod or Halibut with a Lemony Breadcrumb Crust

Rating: Easy   Time: 20 minutes

Suggested Wine: Sparkling white wine

Ingredients:

1 lb skinned fish of your choice   ½ cup melted butter

1 large lemon   Salt and pepper

¾ cup seasoned breadcrumbs

Directions:

Wash and dry the fish filet and cut in half. Season the filets with salt and pepper. Pre-heat the oven to 350 degrees. Place the fish in an oiled baking dish. Sprinkle the breadcrumbs over the fish. Cut the lemon in half and squeeze the juice from ½ a lemon over the breadcrumbs. Then thinly slice the other half of the lemon and lay those slices over the top of the fish. Bake for 20 minutes for thick filets, more than an inch thick. Thin filets will not take as long to bake. Remove the fish, spoon the melted butter on top and serve.

Mussels and Garlic over Linguini

Rating: Moderate   Time: 25 minutes

Suggested Wines: Dry white wines such as chardonnay or pinot grigio

Ingredients:

2-3 dozen fresh mussels (thoroughly cleaned and beards removed)

4 large cloves garlic, chopped	2-3 tbsp olive oil
1 small onion finely diced	½ cup chopped scallions
2 cups dry white wine	½ lb linguini
Salt and pepper to taste	2 large slices of Italian bread
1 tsp chopped parsley	

Directions:

Boil the linguini according to the directions. While the pasta is cooking heat a large stock pot with the olive oil and sauté the onions on medium low heat. Soften but don't brown the onions. After 3 minutes add the garlic and sauté for about 1/2 minute to extract the aroma, but don't brown the garlic. Add the wine and ½ cup of the pasta water, increase the heat to medium high and bring the wine to a simmer. Add the mussels, salt, pepper and cover the pan. Simmer for 4-5 minutes until the mussels open up. Discard any mussels than don't open. Taste the sauce and re-season to your taste. Spoon the mussels and the juices onto the cooked linguini, in individual bowls and sprinkle with the scallions and parsley. Serve with the bread to dip into the sauce. Note: if the pasta is done before the mussels, drain the pasta and pour into a bowl and sprinkle with olive oil to keep the pasta from sticking.

Lobster and Angel Hair Pasta

Rating: Moderate   Time: 30 minutes

Suggested Wine: Chilled chardonnay or pinot grigio

Ingredients:

Two 5-6 oz lobster tails	3 cloves chopped garlic
1 cup white wine, like chardonnay	Salt and pepper for seasoning
1 medium diced onion	1-2 tbsp of olive oil

1 tbsp of parsley, chopped   Juice of one lemon
Parmesan cheese   ½ lb angel hair pasta
Directions:

Bring a large pot of salted water to a boil for the pasta but don't cook the pasta until the lobster is done as angel hair only takes 2-3 minutes to cook. Wash the lobster tails thoroughly. In a medium pot simmer the lobster tails for 12 minutes in salted water and remove the tails to cool saving a cup of the lobster cooking water.

In the same pot, pour out the water, wipe with a paper towel and return it to the stove. Sauté the onions in oil on medium low heat until soft but not brown and add the garlic for about 1 minute. Add the wine, lemon juice and lobster water to the pot and bring to a simmer and reduce by half, season with salt and pepper to taste. Start cooking the pasta. Cut the lobster tails in half and remove the lobster meat (try to remove in one piece) and add to the wine sauce for about a minute just to warm. Drain the pasta and pour into 2 serving bowls. Spoon the sauce and lobster on the pasta and sprinkle with the cheese and parsley. Enjoy!

Lobster – Baked Stuffed with Shrimp or Crab

Lobster can be used to create a very romantic dinner
Rating: Challenging   Time: 1 hour
Suggested Wines: Chilled white wines such as chardonnay and sauvignon blanc
Ingredients:
2 fresh lobsters (1-1/4 to 1-1/2 lbs each)
1 cup of small cooked shrimp or cooked crab meat
1 sleeve of Ritz™ crackers   2 tbsp fresh lemon juice
1 stick of melted butter   Salt and pepper
¼ tsp Old Bay™ seasoning   2 tbsp of white wine or water
Directions:

Heat a large pot of salted water to boil the lobsters or to steam the lobsters by bringing just 4 inches of salted water to boil in the same pot, or use a steaming basket.

While the water is being heated smash the crackers while they are still in the paper wrapping to a rough consistency. Pour the crackers in a mixing bowl and break any large pieces with your hands. Add the seasoning and the salt and pepper to taste. Then add the wine or water and the lemon juice. Mix it with your hands. All the crackers should be damp, if not add more liquid. Next add the shrimp or crab and stir sparingly. Preheat the oven to 350 degrees.

Place the lobsters head first into the pot, steam or boil the lobsters until the shells turn red, about 8 minutes, steaming will take a little longer. Remove the lobsters with tongs and plunge them into cold water in a large mixing bowl or pot. Remove the lobsters with tongs after 3-4 minutes and lay them on paper towels on a cutting board. Once they have cooled enough to touch, lay one lobster on its back so that the legs are pointing up, leaving it on paper towels.

With kitchen shears or a sharp knife, cut a slit in the lobster tails starting at the legs but not all of the way through the shell. You're trying to make a pocket for the stuffing. Spread open the tail with your hands in order to create a pocket. With your hands spread half of the stuffing mix into the pocket. Do the same thing with the 2nd lobster. Drizzle the melted butter over the stuffing. Place the two lobsters with the stuffing face up a large sheet or roasting pan. Place the pan on the middle rack in the oven and bake for 15-17 minutes.

The next portion is optional – after they are cooked turn on the broiler in your oven to high and move the pan closer to the broiler element and broil for about a minute to toast the stuffing mix. Watch it carefully so as not to burn the lobster.

Remove from the oven when cooked, plate and serve with melted butter.

Lobster Macaroni and Cheese

This is a decadent dish

Rating: Moderate   Time: 60 minutes

Suggested Wines: Cold sparkling dry wine or champagne is our favorite

Ingredients:

12-16 oz of cooked lobster meat

8 medium cooked shelled shrimp

2 scallions, chopped

½ yellow onion, diced

¾ cup sharp orange cheddar cheese, shredded

3-4 tbsp of the same cheese reserved for serving

1/3 lb penne or farfalle pasta

Salt and pepper

Olive oil

Directions:

Buy cooked lobster or a fresh whole lobster (about 1-1/4 lbs) and boil it for 15 minutes, cool it and remove the meat. You could also buy 4 lobster tails and boil for 12 minutes, cool and remove the meat.

Cut the lobster meat into bite size pieces. Boil the pasta for 2-3 minutes less than recommended on the package, as you want the pasta to be a little undercooked, but not hard. Oil all sides a medium casserole dish. Pre-heat the oven to 375 degrees. Drain the pasta and pour the pasta into the casserole dish, it's okay if a little pasta water is in the casserole dish. Add the onions, scallions, shrimp and lobster and season with salt and pepper to taste and stir. Spread the cheese over the top of the pasta, stir and bake uncovered on a middle rack for 25-30 minutes or until the cheese is bubbling. Remove from oven and sprinkle the reserved cheese on top, broil for a minute or two to brown the cheese on top.

Lobster Tails and Shrimp, Grilled

Rating: Moderate   Time: 30 minutes

Suggested Wines: Chilled white wines such as pinot grigio or a cold micro beer

Suggested Sides: Make the entire dinner on the grill by grilling zucchini and baking potatoes

Ingredients:

2 lobster tails – 5-8 oz each   Skewers

8 large shrimp shelled/deveined

Marinade

2 tbsp of olive oil   3 tbsp grated parmesan

8 tbsp melted butter   Salt and pepper to taste

¼ tsp dried basil

Directions:

Pre-heat the charcoal or gas grill for 20 minutes or until the grill is hot. Slide the shrimp onto skewers and season with salt and pepper. With kitchen shears cut open the lobster tails to expose the meat, on the leg side but don't cut all of the way through the tails. Run a skewer length wise through the lobster tails, this helps to keep the tails from curling up. Open the shell a little by hand until you hear the shell crack and brush the marinade on the lobster meat inside the shell. Place the lobster tails, outside shell down, on the grill on medium to medium high heat. After about 5 minutes flip the lobster tails and grill the inside (leg side) shell for about 5 minutes. Flip back again onto the outside shell and brush more marinade on the lobster meat. Add the shrimp to the grill and brush with marinade. The shrimp should only take about 2-3 minutes a side. When they are pink on both sides they are done. Brush with marinade regularly. The lobster tails will be done when the meat turns white and is no longer translucent, about 15 minutes in total. Remove the lobster tails and shrimp to a serving plate and pour the remaining marinade on the lobster and shrimp and serve.

Lobster and Shrimp Ravioli with Tarragon Cream Sauce

<u>Rating:</u> Challenging   <u>Time:</u> 45 minutes
<u>Suggested Wines:</u> A chilled dry white such as chardonnay or white Bordeaux
<u>Suggested Sides:</u> A simple side such as an avocado salad or steamed spinach with melted butter
<u>Ingredients:</u>

12 oz cooked lobster meat	Cooking spray
12 small cooked shrimp, shelled	Salt and pepper
2 tbsp fresh tarragon chopped	Parmesan cheese
1 pint half and half or cream	Butter
2 puff pastry sheets	Parchment or baking paper
1 tbsp fresh parsley	

(you can substitute 1 tbsp dried tarragon if you don't have fresh)
<u>Directions for raviolis:</u>

Remove the puff pastry from the freezer to thaw leaving it in its wrapper. Cut the lobster and shrimp into bite size pieces and set aside. Preheat the oven to 375 degrees. Once the puff pastry is thawed roll out one piece of puff pastry with a rolling pin using some flour to keep the pastry from sticking to the cutting board or rolling pin. The puff pastry should be stretched out to about 12 inches by 12 inches. You need to cut 4 squares of roughly all the same size from the sheet of puff pastry. To do this we make a template with a piece paper which we use to trace squares in the puff pastry using a knife or pizza cutter to cut the squares. The squares should be about 6 inches by 6 inches, it's not important to have exact measurements.

On a sheet pan lay a piece of parchment paper and spray both sides with cooking spray to prevent sticking. Lay one piece of puff pastry on the parchment paper and distribute half of the lobster and shrimp on top and season with salt, pepper and fresh parsley. Cover the lobster with another piece of puff pastry to form a ravioli and crimp the sides with a fork that has been dipped in water. Repeat for the second ravioli. Bake the raviolis for 15-20 minutes or until the pastry dough is golden brown on top and bottom. Remove the raviolis to two dinner plates and spoon the tarragon cream sauce (see below) on top and sprinkle with a little parmesan cheese, parsley and serve.

Tarragon Cream Sauce:

While the raviolis are baking you can make the sauce. Heat the half and half and bring to a slow simmer in a sauce pot. Add the tarragon and season the sauce with salt and pepper. Reduce the cream sauce by about 40% to 50% by slow simmering, stirring regularly and don't let it boil over. After it's reduced add 2 tbsp of butter and stir. Taste the sauce and re-season with salt and pepper to your taste. Remove from the heat.

Halibut Roasted with Almonds, Bell Pepper and Onion

This dish is healthy and very tasty. Fresh halibut is probably my favorite fish

Rating: Easy   Time: 30 minutes

Suggested Wines: Chilled sparkling wine such as Prosecco

Ingredients:

12-16 oz fresh halibut, skin removed (or any white fish such as cod or haddock)

½ cup red bell pepper, diced   2 tbsp of olive oil

¼ cup yellow onion, diced   Salt and pepper to taste

¾ cup sliced almonds

Directions:

Pre-heat the oven to 350 degrees. Cut filet in half and brush both sides of the halibut filets with olive oil and place in a baking dish and season with salt and pepper. Pat the sliced almonds on the fish, on all sides. Season the bell pepper and onion with salt and pepper and spoon the bell pepper and onion on top of the fish. Bake for 20 minutes and serve hot.

Shrimp and Creamy Risotto

This creamy flavorful dish with help create a romantic atmosphere with the help of candles

Rating: Moderate   Time: 40 minutes

Suggested wines: chilled sauvignon blanc or pinot grigio

Ingredients:

1 cup risotto (arborio) rice   3 cloves garlic, crushed

3 tbsp olive oil   ½ yellow onion, diced

2 tbsp butter   1 cup half and half

1 cup dry white wine   1 tsp of dried basil
16 oz chicken/vegetable stock   ¼ tsp of dried thyme
12 cooked, shelled medium shrimp   Parmesan cheese
Salt and red pepper flakes
Optional: 2 tbsp of sun dried tomatoes that have been softened and sliced
Directions:

Add the stock and 2 cups of water to a pot and bring to a simmer and reduce to low heat. You'll use this stock to ladle into the rice every couple of minutes.

Heat olive oil in a large nonstick skillet or a large pot over medium heat. Once the oil is hot, but not smoking add the onion and sauté for 2-3 minutes being careful not to brown the onion and then add the rice. Stir the rice constantly for 1 minute (you just want to toast the rice a little, you don't want to brown it). Add the garlic and stir for 1 minute more, being careful not to burn the garlic. Add the wine and 1 cup of the preheated stock and bring to a simmer and season with 1 tsp of salt and 1/4 tsp of red pepper flakes. Reduce heat to medium low as you want a slow simmer. Stir the rice frequently and don't walk away. Add more stock as needed so that the rice never dries out, it should always be a little watery. The cooking process will generally take about 20 minutes. Taste the rice after 20 minutes to see if it is done al dente, or a little firm.

Once the rice is cooked add the cream, thyme and basil. Taste the sauce and re-season if necessary. The sauce should have a little bit of a kick from the red pepper flakes but not too spicy. When the cream starts to simmer slowly, let it simmer for 2-3 minutes more or until the cream is absorbed in the rice and then add the shrimp and butter. Stir the rice, cover the pan and turn off the heat. After 2-3 minutes uncover the pan and let it sit for several minutes uncovered in the pan. This helps to thicken the sauce and allow the rice to absorb more flavor. Sprinkle with cheese and serve. Note that this dish can be made ahead of time and reheated in a microwave oven and tastes even better the next day as long as it's covered and refrigerated.

Clams and Sausage over Fettuccini
Rating: Moderate   Time: 60 minutes
Suggested Wines: A bold dry red such as Chianti, cabernet or pinot noir
Suggested Sides: A small side salad and crusty Italian bread for dipping

Ingredients:

12 -15 littleneck clams, scrubbed and cleaned

1 cup dry white wine   6 – 8 cherry tomatoes cut in half
3 scallions chopped   ½ tsp dried basil
½ yellow onion, sliced thin   Salt
4 cloves garlic, crushed   Red pepper flakes
2 tbsp olive oil   Shredded parmesan cheese
½ lb fettuccini   2 links Italian sausage

Directions:

Heat a stock pot of salted water on high for the pasta. In a medium sauce pan steam the clams in 2 inches of water and a tsp of salt. When the clams have opened up remove the pan from the stove scoop the clams into a bowl and strain the clam water through a strainer into another bowl, as you will use the clam water. Be careful not to overcook clams and they will get tough. Discard any clams that did not open.

Fry the sausages in a large skillet until cooked through. Remove the sausage from the pan and add the garlic and onions and sauté for a minute being careful not to brown them. Start boiling the fettuccini. Add the white wine and clam water to deglaze the skillet. Scrape the bits of meat off the bottom of the pan with a wooden or plastic spatula and bring it to a simmer. Cut the sausage into bite size pieces. Season the wine sauce with salt, basil and red pepper flakes to your taste. Continue to simmer the wine sauce for 10 minutes to reduce and intensify the flavors. During the last 2-3 minutes add the sausage and clams back into the sauce. Cook the pasta until it is al dente. Taste the sauce and re-season and add the tomatoes. Stir the pasta into the white sauce and then pour or spoon it all into a large pasta serving bowl or into individual bowls. Top off with scallions and parmesan cheese and serve.

Crab Stuffed Pasta Shells Southwest Style

This will please the taste buds of anyone who loves crab cakes

Rating: Challenging   Time: 60 minutes
Suggested Wines: Semi dry red wines such as merlot

Ingredients:

10 large pasta shells
Olive oil

Stuffing:

10 oz pre-cooked crab meat
2 shallots, minced
½ cup red bell pepper, minced
2 tbsp mayonnaise

Sauce:

14 -16 oz diced tomatoes
Pinch of cayenne pepper
1 medium yellow onion, diced

½ cup shredded pepper jack cheese

1 tsp spicy brown mustard
1 tsp salt
1 small jalapeno, minced

2 scallions, chopped
2-3 garlic cloves, minced
Salt to taste

Directions:

Place the uncooked pasta shells in a bowl to separate them with your hands before you boil them. In a large stock pot boil the shells according to package directions, but remove the pot from the heat 2-3 minutes before they are fully cooked and save ¼ cup of the pasta water for later. Drain the pasta in a colander and pour them into a large bowl pan and add a couple tbsp of olive oil to coat the shells, stirring gently. This will prevent the shells from sticking while they cool. Mix all the stuffing ingredients together in a mixing bowl.

Mix all of the sauce ingredients together in a separate mixing bowl. Pre-heat the oven to 350 degrees. Select a casserole dish that will hold the shells upright while you bake them and fit snugly in the dish. Grease the dish with a little olive oil in the bottom and sides. Fill the shells one at a time with the crab meat stuffing and place the stuffed shells in the casserole dish, stuffing side up. Pour the reserved pasta water in the bottom of the dish. Once the casserole dish is filled with stuffed shells pour the sauce over the top of the shells and bake for 25-30 minutes, on a middle rack in the oven. Remove the dish from the oven and sprinkle with pepper jack cheese, let cool for 5 minutes and serve.

Crab Stuffed Beefsteak Tomatoes

Amaze your partner with this simple and delicious dish

Rating: Moderate   Time: 30 minutes

Suggested Wines: Semi dry red wines such as merlot or a semi dry white such as soave

Ingredients:
2 very large beefsteak tomatoes or 4 large tomatoes
Stuffing:

8 oz pre-cooked crab meat

1 shallot, finely minced

2 scallions, chopped

¼ cup red bell pepper, minced

1-½ tbsp mayonnaise

1 tsp spicy brown mustard

Salt and pepper

Olive oil

Topping:
¼ cup shredded mozzarella or parmesan cheese
Directions:

   Pre-heat the oven to 350 degrees.   Cut the tops off of the tomatoes and scoop out the core and seeds with a melon baller or spoon. Cut a small thin slice off of the bottoms of the tomatoes if they will not stand upright on their own. Save the removed pulp for sauce. Season the inside of the tomatoes with salt and pepper and drizzle a little olive oil inside. Mix all of the stuffing ingredients together in a mixing bowl and taste. Add more salt and pepper to your taste. Spoon the stuffing into the tomatoes, mounding the stuffing. In a small casserole dish or pan with sides to hold the tomatoes upright drizzle a little oil. Drizzle the top of the tomatoes with olive oil. Bake for about 15 minutes. Sprinkle the tops with cheese and bake 5 minutes more until the cheese melts. Serve hot or warm. This dish also tastes great the next day served cold. Enjoy.

Trout Baked with Vegetables

This is a very unique way to cook your freshly caught or purchased trout

Rating: Challenging   Time: 60 minutes

Suggested Wines: Chilled dry whites such as chardonnay or pinot grigio

Ingredients:

2 fresh whole trout

Olive oil

Butter

½ cup flour

Salt and pepper

½ tsp dried thyme

Vegetables:

1 small zucchini, diced

9 large green olives with pimentos

1 medium yellow onion, sliced

8 cherry tomatoes, cut in half

1 small red bell pepper, cut in strips

1 small yellow squash, diced

Garnish: 4 thin slices fresh lemon

Directions:

Preheat the oven to 350 degrees. Add all of the vegetables to a mixing bowl and season with salt and pepper. Cut the trout's belly open from the gills down to the end of the tail with a sharp knife. Lightly dust the trout's skin with flour and salt and pepper. Season the body cavity with salt and pepper but not flour. In a medium non-stick skillet melt 2 tbsp of butter and 2 tbsp of olive oil on medium heat. Fry one trout skin side down for about a minute or two just to brown it and flip it to fry the other side, skin side. Now flip it so that the belly side of the trout is face down and open in the pan, open the fish as much as possible by pressing down with a spatula. Fry for a couple of minutes and remove the pan from the burner and transfer the trout to a cutting board belly side up. Repeat the process with the second trout, adding more butter and oil to the skillet as needed.

With a knife and fork you should be able to remove back bones and all of the attached bones as well as the tail from the trout. It's up to you whether to remove the head or not. Lay both fish back side down, spreading open the body cavity, in a flat baking pan or casserole that has been oiled with 1-2 tbsp of olive oil to prevent sticking. Spoon the vegetables into the body cavity and around the pan. Sprinkle the body cavity with a tsp of olive oil and bake for 15-20 minutes or until the fish is cooked through. Remove from oven and transfer each fish to a plate skin side down spooning the vegetables into the body cavity, and serve. Garnish the plates with the remaining lemon.

Grouper with Pineapple

Rating: Moderate   Time: 30 minutes
Suggested Wines: A cold white wine such as pinot grigio or sparkling wine
Ingredients:

12-16 oz. grouper filet (or cod)	½ tsp jalapeno pepper, diced
1 small can diced pineapple	2 tsp olive oil
¼ bell pepper, diced	Salt and pepper
8 large shrimp, cooked and cleaned	

Directions:

Pre-heat the oven to 350 degrees. Rinse and dry the fish with paper towels.

Season the fish with salt and pepper. Oil a baking dish and place the fish filet on the oil. Pour the can of pineapple over the fish, including all the juices. Sprinkle the diced peppers on top.

Bake for 15 minutes if the filets are thin (less than an inch) and for 20 minutes if the filets are thicker. Turn off the oven when the fish is done and open the door. Place the shrimp on top of the pineapple, close the oven door for 2-3 minutes to warm the shrimp. Remove the dish and transfer the filets to dinner plates and serve.

Flounder Baked with a Mustard Horseradish Topping

Rating: Moderate   Time: 30 minutes
Suggested Wines: Chilled semi dry whites such as sauvignon blanc
Ingredients:
12-16 oz flounder / sole or other white flesh fish such haddock, skinned
½ cup Dijon mustard   ¼ lb dried / fresh egg noodles
½ cup sour cream   3 scallions, chopped
1 or 2 tbsp prepared horseradish   Salt and pepper
Directions:

Pre-heat oven to 350 degrees. Wash the fish and dry with paper towels and season with salt and pepper. In a mixing bowl combine mustard, sour cream and horseradish. Spoon enough onto the fish to coat it and save the rest for the sauce. Bake the fish for about 15 minutes if the filets are pretty thin, if the fish is reasonably thick - 1 inch or more bake for about 20 minutes. While the fish is baking boil the egg noodles according to the package directions. Drain the noodles and pour them into a casserole bowl. Spoon on the remaining Dijon mustard sauce and cover. When the fish is done, cut into 2 portions. Spoon a bed of egg noodles on 2 dinner plates and place the fish on top and serve. Sprinkle with chopped scallions.

Poultry, Beef and Pork Entrées

(For a simple dry rub recipe for meat see the last page of the Index)

Chicken Sautéed in Marsala Wine on a Bed of Orzo

Note that you can substitute veal cutlets or boneless turkey if you prefer

Rating: Moderate

Time: 30 Minutes

Suggested Wines: A bold dry red such as Italian Chianti or Barolo

Ingredients:

2 chicken breasts, boneless and skinless

6 cremini or white mushrooms, sliced thin

½ cup orzo pasta   Salt and pepper

1 medium yellow onion, diced   Parmesan cheese

3 garlic cloves, chopped   2 tbsp parsley, chopped

1 cup Marsala wine   Olive oil and butter

Directions:

Pound the chicken breast thin with a meat mallet, placing the chicken in a zipper plastic bag and pounding thin, less than 1 inch thick. Season them with salt and pepper on both sides. Fry the chicken in 2 tbsp of olive oil and 1 tbsp butter on medium heat about 4 minutes a side in a non-stick skillet. Remove the chicken to a plate and add the onions and mushrooms to the skillet, adding 1 tbsp olive oil and 1 tbsp butter to the pan. Sauté for 5 minutes, try not to brown the onions by reducing the heat if necessary.

Start a small pot of salted water boiling for the pasta. Add the garlic to the frying pan with the onions for 30 seconds. Turn off the burner and add the wine carefully. Turn the burner back on and deglaze the pan, scrapping the bits of meat off the bottom with a spatula and season the wine sauce with salt and pepper.   Simmer the wine until it has reduced by 50% and then add the chicken back into the pan along with the parsley. Heat the chicken on both sides for a minute or two per side and turn off the heat.   Taste the sauce and re-season to your liking. Cover the frying pan to keep warm. Boil ½ cup of orzo according to the directions on the package. Drain the pasta and spoon the orzo onto 2 plates and place the chicken on top, spooning some of the sauce and mushrooms on the chicken. Sprinkle with cheese and serve.

Breast of Chicken with a Spicy Dijon Sauce Over Rice

Rating: Moderate   Time: 40 minutes
Suggested Wines: Either a semi dry red such as merlot or zinfandel or a dry white such as chardonnay
Ingredients:
2 boneless, skinless chicken breasts

½ cup basmati rice	Butter
½ yellow onion, diced	Olive oil
3 scallions, chopped.	Salt and pepper

Sauce:

4 tbsp Dijon mustard	1 tsp olive oil
2 tbsp mayonnaise	½ tsp hot sauce
2 tbsp sour cream	Salt and pepper

Directions:

   Start boiling the rice using the package directions. After 5 minutes of boiling add the onions to the boiling rice and season with salt and pepper. Place one chicken breast in a zipper plastic bag or between 2 sheets of plastic wrap and pound thin (less than 1 in. thick) with a meat mallet, remove and pound the second chicken breast thin. Heat a large non-stick skillet on medium heat with 2-3 tbsp olive oil. Season the chicken on both sides with salt and pepper and place both pieces in the skillet when the oil is hot but not smoking. Brown on one side for about 4 minutes and flip and brown on the other side for another 4 minutes.

   While the chicken is cooking make the sauce in a glass measuring cup or bowl. Add all the ingredients for the sauce and stir or whisk. Cover the sauce bowl with a microwave safe cover and microwave for 60-90 seconds, just to heat it up. Don't boil the sauce. Remove the chicken to a plate when cooked and cover loosely with aluminum foil or pot cover to rest for a minute or two. When the rice has absorbed all of the water turn off the heat and add 1 tbsp of butter and stir. Taste the sauce and re-season according to your taste with salt, pepper or hot sauce. Spoon the rice onto 2 dinner plates. Place the chicken breasts on top of the rice and spoon the sauce over the chicken and rice. Sprinkle the chopped scallions on top and serve.

Chicken Breasts with a Crunchy Maple Topping

An easy and quick recipe for chicken with an awesome Vermont flavor

Rating: Moderate   Time: 20 minutes

Suggested Wines: White Bordeaux or pinot grigio

Suggested Sides: Maple flavored brussel sprouts and garlic smashed potatoes

Ingredients:

2 chicken breasts, skinless and boneless

1 cup mini wheat cereal, maple & brown sugar flavor (or breadcrumbs)

Maple syrup   Olive oil

Salt and pepper

Directions:

Pound the chicken breasts thin between two pieces of plastic wrap or in a zip lock type bag (less than 1inch thick). Season both sides with salt and pepper. Add 2 tbsp olive oil to a non-stick medium skillet and turn burner on medium. When the oil is hot but not smoking place the breasts in the skillet and brown on one side for 4 minutes and flip and brown the other side for 4 minutes and remove immediately from the skillet to an casserole dish.

Turn on the oven broiler. Drizzle each breast with a little maple syrup. Break up the mini wheat cereal with your fingers and pile it on top of the two chicken breasts. Place the dish under the broiler about 2 inches from the heating element and watch it carefully.   Broil just long enough to crisp up the cereal and toast it a little. Remove to a plate and drizzle 1 tsp maple syrup on top of the cereal crust and serve.

Chicken and Shrimp Fettuccini in a Creamy Sauce

This rich dish with a lighted candle will impress your special someone

Rating: Challenging   Time: 45 minutes

Suggested Wines: Your favorite dry red or white wine will go well with this dish

Ingredients:

¼ lb chicken strips (2 in. long by ¼ in. thick)

½ cup of dry white wine (or chicken / vegetable stock)

8 medium cooked & cleaned shrimp   3 garlic cloves, chopped

1 medium yellow onion, chopped

¼ of a red bell pepper, chopped

Olive oil

½ lb of linguini or spaghetti

1 cup half and half

Salt and red pepper flakes

½ tsp dried basil

¼ tsp dried thyme

1 tbsp butter

½ cup Parmesan cheese

½ cup chopped fresh parsley

Directions:

Heat salted water for the pasta in a large pot on high heat. Heat 2 tbsp of olive oil in a large non stick skillet on medium heat. Season the chicken with salt and pepper and then fry the chicken strips until brown on all sides. Remove the chicken to a plate. Add more olive oil as needed and sauté the onions and bell pepper for 5 minutes until softened, don't brown them. Add the garlic for about a minute more. Remove the pan from the burner and add the white wine or stock to the pan to deglaze it, stir the bits off of the bottom of the skillet with a wooden spoon or spatula. Season the mix with a pinch of red pepper flakes, basil, 1 tsp salt and thyme. Simmer on medium or medium low for 2-3 minutes or until the liquid is reduced by 50%.

Boil the pasta according to the package directions. Add the half and half to the skillet and simmer slowly or the half and half will separate. After simmering for about 3-4 minutes add the cooked chicken and shrimp into the pan. Simmer for another couple of minutes and add the butter and parmesan cheese until melted and lower the heat to low. The cheese will thicken the sauce. Taste the sauce and re-season with salt and pepper to your liking. The sauce should have a little heat from the red pepper flakes. Turn off the heat and cover the skillet until the pasta is done. When the pasta is done, drain it and spoon into 2 serving bowls or plates and spoon the sauce and chicken over the pasta, sprinkle with fresh parsley and more cheese and serve.

Chicken Breasts Stuffed with Fontina Cheese and Prosciutto

This awesome dish combines the wonderful taste of fontina and chicken and will impress your partner

Rating: Challenging   Time: 45-60 minutes

Suggested Wine: Dry reds such as Chianti, cabernet, shiraz and Burgundy

Ingredients:

2 boneless skinless chicken breasts pounded thin, less than 1 inch thick

4 cloves garlic, crushed
½ medium yellow onion, diced
4 slices of fontina cheese
4 slices of prosciutto
¼ tsp dried basil
Salt and pepper
28-32 oz diced tomatoes
12-16 oz baby spinach leaves, stems removed

1 cup dry red wine
Parmesan cheese
3 scallions, chopped
Olive oil
¼ lb of orecchiette or rotelle pasta
Toothpicks

Directions:

Preheat the oven to 350 and start heating the salted water for the pasta in a large pot.   Heat a large non-stick skillet with 3 tbsp of olive oil on medium heat. Cut the chicken breasts in half, after pounding them thin, so that you have 4 slices or medallions about the same size. Season the chicken with salt, pepper and dried basil. Brown the chicken on both sides in the hot oil, about 3 minutes a side and remove from the skillet to a plate and cover.

Reduce heat to medium low and add the onion to the skillet and sauté for about 2-3 minutes and then add the garlic for another 30 seconds, trying not to brown them. Move your skillet away from the burner and pour in the wine. Return the pan to the burner and deglaze the pan, scrapping the meat bits off the bottom. After a couple of minutes add tomatoes and juices. Season the sauce with a basil, salt and pepper and taste and re-season to your taste. Add 90% of chopped spinach to the tomato sauce and simmer.

On a cutting board, make a "sandwich" with the chicken by placing one cooked chicken breast on the board, then add a slice of fontina, then the prosciutto, then a few spinach leaves and then another slice of fontina and finally add the second chicken breast on top. Hold it together with a couple of toothpicks. Repeat with the other chicken pieces and transfer the "sandwiches" to a casserole dish that has been oiled. Spoon about a cup of sauce over the chicken. Bake the chicken in the oven for about 10 minutes.

Start boiling the pasta after you place the chicken in the oven. Strain the pasta and then pour it all into the sauce and stir, continue to heat on low. Spoon some pasta and sauce on a dinner plate and make a circle in the middle and with your tongs transfer a chicken "sandwich" to the circle on the plate and remove the toothpicks. This dish is also referred to as chicken napoleon. Sprinkle with scallions and parmesan and serve.

Chicken and Broccolini in a White Wine Sauce

Rating: Easy   Time: 30 minutes

Suggested Wine: Pinot grigio

Substitution: You can substitute a small turkey breast if you prefer

Ingredients:

2 boneless skinless chicken breasts

½ lb rigatoni or penne pasta   6 cherry tomatoes cut in half

4 cloves garlic, crushed   1 cup dry white wine

1 medium yellow onion, diced   1 pinch red pepper flakes

1 bunch broccolini   Parmesan cheese

½ tsp dried basil (or fresh)   1 tbsp chopped parsley

Salt and pepper   Olive oil

Directions:

 Cut the chicken breasts into bite sized pieces, season with salt, pepper and dried basil. Cook the macaroni according to the directions on the package, al dente. Cut the tough end of the broccolini off and discard. Rinse broccilini and cut the stems from the crowns. While the macaroni is boiling heat a large skillet with 2 tbsp of olive oil over medium heat. Fry the chicken in the skillet until brown on all sides, about 5-6 minutes.   Remove the chicken from the skillet to a bowl and reduce the heat to medium low. Add 2 tbsp of oil to the skillet as well as the onion and broccolini stems and sauté for 5 minutes, stirring frequently. Add the garlic to the skillet for a minute, but don't brown the garlic. Add the wine (away from the burner), red pepper flakes, broccolini crowns and chicken and simmer for 5-8 minutes. Taste the sauce and re-season with salt, pepper or basil according to your liking. Add the tomatoes for a minute or two. Drain the pasta and pour it into the skillet or large pasta bowl with the chicken wine sauce, stir to combine the wine sauce with the pasta. Spoon into pasta bowls and sprinkle with parmesan cheese, parsley and serve.

Chicken Braised in Wine Sauce over Egg Noodles

Rating: Easy   Time: 60-75 minutes

Suggested Wines: Dry red such as pinot noir or cabernet sauvignon

Bread: A good crusty bread or biscuits

Ingredients:

2 whole chicken legs   3-4 cloves garlic, crushed

12-14 oz diced tomatoes
1 celery stalk, chopped
½ yellow onion, sliced
6-8 baby pearl onions, peeled
8-10 baby carrots
2 cups dry red wine for braising

Salt and pepper
Olive oil
¼ tsp dried thyme
8 oz. egg noodles or fettuccini
Chopped scallions & parsley

Directions:

In a large stock pot heat 2-3 tbsp of olive oil over medium heat. Cut the thighs off of the chicken legs leaving the skin on both. Season the 4 pieces of chicken with salt and pepper and add to the pot once the oil is hot but not smoking. Brown the chicken on one side for 2-3 minutes, turn and brown the other side for about 3 minutes. Add the garlic, celery and onion to the pot for 1 minute, being careful not to burn the garlic. Move the pot away from the burner and add the wine to deglaze the pot, scrapping the bits of chicken off of the bottom of the pot. Now add the diced tomatoes, thyme, salt and pepper and simmer the chicken and sauce for about 20 minutes with the pot partially covered. The simmer should be a medium to low simmer, adjust the heat accordingly.

Add the pearl onions and baby carrots and simmer for another 20 minutes. You may need to add water to the pot if there is significant evaporation. The chicken pieces should be mostly covered but not submerged. Turn off the heat and cover the pot and let the chicken absorb the juices. Taste the sauce and re-season to your liking. You can also remove the chicken skins now, it's your preference.

Start the noodles as the chicken rests in the pot. Boil the noodles according to the directions on the package. Once cooked, strain the noodles and then pour the noodles into a large pasta bowl or platter. With a slotted spoon, spoon the chicken and veggies over the noodles. Then spoon some of the tomato sauce over the top and sprinkle with chopped parsley or chopped scallions.

Chicken Cutlets Italian Style

Rating: Easy   Time: 20 minutes
Suggested Wines: Whites such as pinot grigio or soave
Ingredients:
2 chicken breasts, skinless and boneless

4 tbsp mozzarella cheese, shredded
1 large egg
2 cloves of whole garlic, crushed
½ tsp dried basil
Parmesan cheese

Breadcrumbs
Salt and pepper
Olive oil
4-6 fresh basil leaves, chopped

Directions:

Pound the chicken breasts thin between two pieces of plastic wrap or in a zip lock bag (less than 1 inch thick). Season both sides with salt and pepper. Add 4 tbsp olive oil to a non-stick medium skillet and turn burner on medium. Pour 1/2 cup of breadcrumbs on a plate and season with dried basil, salt and pepper. Crack the egg into a small bowl and scramble it with a fork. When the oil is hot, dip each cutlet into the egg wash first and then into the breadcrumbs (both sides) and then lay in the skillet. Brown the cutlets for 4 minutes and flip them and brown the other side for 4 more minutes.

Add more olive oil if the skillet starts to go dry. Add the garlic and turn off the burner and remove the skillet from the stove. Sprinkle the mozzarella cheese on top of each cutlet and cover the skillet with a cover or foil until the cheese melts. Transfer the cutlets to 2 dinner plates, sprinkle with parmesan cheese, fresh basil and serve.

Chicken with a Creamy Parmesan Cheese Sauce

Rating: Moderate   Time: 40 minutes
Suggested Wines: Cold chardonnay or pinot grigio
Ingredients:

4 chicken thighs, with skin
1 cup half and half
½ medium yellow onion, chopped
3 cloves garlic, crushed
1 cup half and half or cream
1 tbsp corn starch (or flour)
Salt and pepper

½ tsp dried thyme
¼ tsp dried rosemary
¼ tsp dried sage
Butter
Olive oil
2 tbsp parmesan cheese
2 scallions, chopped

6-8 medium mushrooms, white or cremini, sliced

Directions:

Simmer the chicken thighs in enough salted water to cover them for 20-30 minutes in a covered pot, or until the meat starts to separate from the bone.

Remove the chicken to a dish to cool and remove the skin and bones and discard. Cut the chicken into bite size pieces. Pour the remaining chicken stock from the pot into a measuring cup or bowl. In the same sauce pot add 2 tbsp butter and 2 tbsp olive oil and heat on medium. When the butter starts to melt add the onion and mushrooms and sauté for 5 minutes, trying not to burn them. Add the garlic and sauté for 30 seconds and then add ¼ cup of chicken stock and the half and half, simmer until the liquid is reduced by about half. Add the rosemary, thyme and sage and stir the pot. Season with salt and pepper to your taste.

In a cup, add the corn starch and 1/4 cup of water and stir with a fork until the corn starch is fully dissolved. Add the corn starch thickener to the sauce and stir constantly until the sauce thickens. Add the parmesan cheese and stir to incorporate with the sauce. Then add the chicken pieces to the sauce. Taste the sauce and re-season to your liking. Sprinkle the mix with scallions and stir, as soon as it comes to a simmer again, stir it and turn off the heat and cover the pot for 5-8 minutes, leaving it on the burner. This allows the flavors to develop and thickens the sauce. Serve when ready.

Chicken Quesadilla

Rating: Easy   Time: 30 minutes
Beverage: a cold crisp wine like a pinot grigio or a cold Mexican beer with a lime wedge
Recommendations: Substitute turkey if you like and serve with Mexican rice
Ingredients:
½ lb. of chicken strips (2 in. long by ¼ in. thick)
2 cups shredded Monterey Jack cheese
4 large burrito tortillas   2-3 tbsp olive oil
1 medium jalapeno, chopped   Salt and pepper
1 jar of your favorite mild salsa   Cumin powder (optional)
1 cup chopped black olives   Garlic powder
1 pint of sour cream
Directions:
Heat the oil over medium heat in a small skillet. Season the chicken strips with salt, pepper, cumin and garlic powder. When oil is hot but not smoking add the chicken and stir fry for about 5 minutes or until done, stirring frequently.

Remove the chicken from the heat. In a medium to large frying pan heat the burritos on medium-low heat with NO oil in the pan. All you want to do is warm the shells until they are soft, about 10 seconds per side. Heat them one at a time and remove and stack on a plate.

After heating the burritos, place one burrito on a cutting board. Spread half of the cooked chicken evenly over the burrito. Then spread the jalapeno, olives and 1-2 tbsp of salsa over the chicken. Taste the jalapeno and if it's extra hot you may wish to use less. Season with salt and pepper and then spread the cheese on top. Cover with a second burrito tortilla. Cut the quesadillas into 4 wedges, add a tbsp of sour cream on top of each wedge and serve. Do they same thing with the other two burritos. You can make them ahead of time (without the sour cream) and warm them in a 300 degree oven for 10 minutes on a cookie sheet and add the sour cream on top after you've heated them to warm, not hot. Serve some salsa on the side at the table.

Chicken or Turkey Pot Pie

Rating: Challenging   Time: 60 minutes
Suggested Wines: Chilled whites such as chenin blanc or pinot grigio
Ingredients:

3 cups cooked chicken or turkey, diced
2 medium carrots, diced   2 tsp of corn starch or flour
1 stalk of celery, diced   1 tbsp fresh parsley
1 med. yellow / sweet onion, diced   1 sheet puff pastry dough, thawed
¼ cup frozen peas   Salt and pepper
½ red bell pepper, diced   Dry rub spices, any brand
3-4 cloves garlic, crushed   Olive oil
14-16 oz chicken broth
6-8 medium fresh mushrooms, cremini or white
1 egg/1 tsp of water whisked-egg wash
2 oven safe ramekin bowls (about 5-1/2" x 2") or soup bowls
Optional: hot sauce added to the chicken and veggie sauce
Directions:

Lightly season the chicken with the dry rub in a small bowl. Add 2 tbsp of olive oil to a large sauce pan and sauté the carrots, onions, mushrooms, bell pepper, peas and celery for about 5 minutes on medium low heat until the vegetables are soft, trying not to brown the vegetables. Add the garlic and sauté for about 30 seconds. Season with salt and pepper and add the chicken broth and the chicken pieces. Add some hot sauce now if you prefer a spicy pot pie. Simmer until the broth is reduced by half.

Create a thickener by adding the corn starch and ½ cup of water to a bowl and stir with a fork until it's fully dissolved. Add the thickener to the pot and stir and bring to a simmer to fully thicken the sauce, stirring frequently. Once the sauce has thickened, remove the skillet from the burner and add the parsley. Cool the mix in a mixing bowl in the refrigerator. After the chicken has cooled pre-heat oven to 400 degrees. Taste and re-season the chicken.

Using a rolling pin roll out the puff pastry to about ¼ inch thick, be sure to use some flour to keep the dough from sticking to the rolling pin. Using the ramekin or soup bowls invert one bowl onto the dough. With a sharp knife cut a circle in the dough about 2 inches wider in circumference than the bowl outline. Butter (or spray with cooking spray) each bowl inside on the bottom and sides. Spoon the cooled chicken mix, including the sauce into the first bowl, bringing the mix right up to the top edge and cover the bowl with a dough circle. Press the dough to the outside of the bowl. Cut a couple of slits (2-3 inches long) in the top of the dough to act as air vents. Brush the egg wash on the top. Repeat the process for the second ramekin bowl.

Place both bowls on a cookie sheet, cover them with aluminum foil and bake for about 15 minutes, remove the foil and bake for another 10 minutes or until the dough is golden brown. Remove the bowls from oven and let cool. Be sure the crust is a nice rich brown color. The baking time will vary based on the size of your ramekin bowls. Enjoy.

Game Hen or Chicken Grilled Butterfly Style
Rating: Challenging   Time: 45 minutes
Suggested Beverages: Cold micro brew beer or sauvignon blanc wine
Ingredients:
1 large game hen or 1 small whole chicken
Dry rub
Optional: your favorite BBQ sauce
Directions:

To butterfly the hen, remove the giblets from the inside. Lay the hen breast side down on a cutting board. You need to cut the backbone out.

With a pair of kitchen shears cut along both sides of the backbone from the neck all the way down through the tail and remove the backbone. Turn the hen over – skin side up and press down between the breasts with your hand to break the keel bone, as this will allow the hen to lay flat on the grill. Preheat a gas or charcoal grill until the grill is hot. Season the hen on both sides liberally with the dry rub. Lay the hen out on the grill breast side down (the legs and thighs should be all touching the grill) and reduce the flame to medium. Brown the breast side for 5-10 minutes until the skin has grill marks, but not blackened.

Flip the hen over and close the grill cover and reduce the heat to about 375 degrees. It should take 20-35 minutes to roast a hen or chicken once you lower the cover, depending on the size of the bird and the temperature of your grill. Check the temperature after 20 minutes with an instant thermometer in the thigh and remove the hen when it registers 180 degrees or lower depending on your preference. You can brush on barbeque sauce one or two times during the roasting process, if you like. Remove the hen to a platter and rest for 5-10 minutes to redistribute the juices.

Cut the hen in half and serve for two.

Game Hen Roasted Whole on the Grill

Rating: Moderate   Time: 1 hour
Suggested Wines: Chilled dry wines such as chardonnay and pinot blanc
Ingredients:
1 large game hen with giblets removed, washed and dried

Dry rub for poultry	1 tsp ground sage
10-14 oz of chicken stock	Salt and pepper
1 medium onion, diced	1/2 cup of uncooked rice
1 bay leaf	

Thickener:
1 tbsp of corn starch or flour stirred and dissolved into ½ cup of water
Directions:
Pre-heat the grill with the cover down to 450 degrees. Sprinkle the hen with the dry rub liberally and place it in a small roasting pan. Place the roasting pan on the grill and close the cover for about 5 minutes watching for flame flair ups and then reduce the grill to medium heat (350 degrees). Heat the chicken stock in a sauce pot for basting, add the onions and bring the stock to a simmer on the

stove burner. You will use some of the stock for basting and some for gravy.
Add the neck to the sauce. (Optional: chop up the giblets and add to the stock).
Season the stock with sage, salt and pepper and one bay leaf. Cook the rice
according the directions on the package.

After roasting for 10 to 15 minutes baste the hen with the hot chicken stock
with a brush. Baste again after 10 more minutes. After the hen has roasted for
30 minutes in total, check to see if the hen is done with a thermometer placed in
the breast (180 degrees or less if you prefer).

When the hen is done remove the roasting pan from the grill. Remove the
hen to a plate or cutting board and let rest for 10 minutes before cutting to help
retain the juices in the bird. Meanwhile scrape the roasting pan with a spatula
and pour the juices and bits of meat into the pot with the chicken stock. Bring the
stock to a boil and simmer for a few minutes and remove the bay leaf and neck.
Stir the thickener thoroughly to fully dissolve the corn starch (otherwise you will
get lumps) and pour and stir the thickener into the stock to thicken and make a
gravy. Bring the gravy back to a boil stirring continually and then turn off the
heat. Taste the gravy and re-season with salt and pepper to your taste. Cut the
hen in half so that you have a leg, wing and half a breast on each half. Plate the
halves and spoon over with some gravy and serve over rice.

Duck Breasts with Raspberry Sauce

*This is an elegant main course for those with a sweet tooth. Duck is one of my
favorite meats.*

Rating: Moderate   Time: 20 minutes

Suggested Wines: Both reds and whites will work with this dish, cabernet or
pinot grigio

Notes: This recipe works best cooking on a grill pan or on a gas grill outside

Ingredients:

2 duck breasts (6 – 8 oz each) with skin on

½ cup raspberry preserves   1 tbsp olive oil

½ cup fresh raspberries   Salt and pepper

1 tbsp butter   (Optional: 1 tbsp of brandy)

Directions:

Score the skin side of the duck breasts, this means cutting thin slits in the
duck skin in a crisscross pattern making sure the cuts are only skin deep. In a

small sauce pan melt the butter on medium heat and then add the raspberry preserves and take the pan off of the stove to add the brandy, to avoid a fire. Reduce the heat on the pan to a low simmer to thicken for about 5 minutes, season with salt and pepper to your taste and then cover and turn the heat off.

Add the oil to a grill pan, just enough to lightly coat the bottom of the pan (or grill the duck outside on a gas grill). Season the duck breasts with salt and pepper. Heat the pan on medium heat. Once the pan is hot but not smoking, place the breasts in the pan, skin down and sear the skin. Searing the skin will render out quite a bit of fat. Pour off the fat into a bowl and later discard as many times as you need to keep the fat to a minimum. Once the skin side has been browned (about 5 minutes) turn the duck breasts with tongs and brown the other side for about 5 minutes, for medium rare. Sear a little longer if you prefer duck medium. I don't recommend cooking duck past medium as it gets tough.

Remove the breast to a plate to rest for about 5 minutes. Then transfer the duck breasts to dinner plates and spoon over the raspberry sauce and the fresh raspberries on top of the sauce.

Filet Mignon with Shrimp in a Peppery Cream Sauce

Rating: Moderate   Time: 30 minutes

Suggested Wines: A full bodied red wine with a little aging such as a quality cabernet sauvignon or pinot noir

Suggested Side Dishes: potatoes au gratin and steamed broccoli with hollandaise sauce

Ingredients:

2 medallions of filet mignon 1-1/2 to 2 inches thick (about 6-8 oz each)

8 large raw shrimp, deveined & peeled

1 cup of cream or half and half	Butter
10 whole peppercorns	Salt and pepper
1 large shallot diced	1 tbsp of chopped parsley
Olive oil	

Optional: 4 medium thin sliced fresh white or brown mushrooms

Directions:

Remove the meat from the refrigerator for 20 minutes to bring to room temperature. Season the medallions on both sides with salt and pepper. Heat 1 tbsp of olive oil and 1 tbsp of butter in a medium grill pan (about 2 inches deep or more) or skillet on medium. When the oil is hot add the meat to the pan. The meat should sizzle a little but there should be very little smoke, lower the heat if there's much smoke. After 4-5 minutes on one side turn the meat and pan fry 4-5 minutes on the other side, you should have some charring on each side of the steaks. The meat should be medium rare at this point, however the length of time to pan grill the medallions depends on the thickness of the meat. If you like you can test for doneness of the meat with a meat thermometer to the temperature that you prefer. Remove the cooked fillets to a plate and tightly cover with aluminum foil and let rest until the sauce is done, the meat will continue to cook.

After removing the meat from the pan add the raw shrimp to the pan and pan fry shrimp until the shrimp are pink throughout, add more oil if you need it. Remove the shrimp to a bowl.

Add 1 tbsp of butter and 2 tbsp of oil to the pan and reduce the heat to medium low. Add the mushrooms to the pan for 3-4 minutes and then add the shallots. Sauté the shallots and mushrooms at a low temperature, you do not want to brown the shallots. This brings out the sweetness of the shallots. After about 2 or 3 minutes add the cream and scrape the pan with a wooden spatula to loosen the meat bits from the pan. Adjust the temperature of the pan to achieve a low simmer. If you simmer the cream too high it may separate. Season the cream with salt and pepper. Add the whole peppercorns to the cream. Slowly simmer the cream until it's reduced by about 40-50% and stir constantly. Add a tsp of butter to the cream and whisk it until it melts, remove the pan from the heat. Move the filet mignon medallions to individual plates or a serving dish. Place the shrimp on top and pour the cream sauce on each. Garnish each steak with parsley and serve.

Steak Grilled with Mushrooms

Rating: Easy   Time: 30 minutes
Suggested Wines: Dry reds such as Chianti and Burgundy

Ingredients:

2 - 6 oz steaks, strip or ribeye
6-8 fresh mushrooms, sliced
½ cup diced yellow onions

2 tbsp of olive oil
1-2 tbsp of Worstershire sauce
Salt and pepper to taste

Directions:

Remove the steak from the refrigerator to a plate 10-20 minutes before grilling and season with salt and pepper.

In a small skillet heat 2 tbsp of olive oil over medium heat. When the oil is hot add the mushrooms. Do NOT stir the mushrooms but allow them to sit untouched for about 3 minutes so that they brown but don't burn. Once they are browned on one side, flip the mushrooms with a spatula and then toss in the onions on top and cook for another 2-3 minutes without stirring (adding more oil if you need to) and then add the Worstershire sauce and heat for another 2 minutes. Stir the mushrooms and onions and turn off the heat, but leave the skillet on the burner to stay warm. Taste the mushrooms and season with salt and pepper to your liking. Add more Worstershire based on your tastes and preferences. Cover the mushrooms to keep them warm.

Prepare to grill the steaks on a gas or charcoal grill or on the stove. If on the stove: In a non-stick grill pan or skillet add a little olive oil to keep the steaks from sticking and heat the pan on medium heat. When the oil is hot but not smoking place the steaks in the pan. If on the grill: Thoroughly clean the grill and heat to high for 15-20 minutes.

Grill the steaks for 4-5 minutes and turn and grill the other side for 4-5 minutes for medium rare, it may take a little longer on a charcoal or gas grill depending on how hot the grill was when you started. Also, if your steaks are thick it may take a little longer to grill to medium rare. If your partner prefers their steak medium to well done, you can remove the first steak now and allow the second steak to grill for another minute or two. Remove the steaks to a plate and cover with aluminum foil and allow them to rest for 5-10 minutes. Cutting them before allowing them to rest would release all the juices and is not a good idea. If you grill the steaks in a pan scrape the pan juices and particles into the mushroom pan and stir.

When you're ready to eat, spoon half of the mushroom and Worstershire sauce mixture over each steak and serve.

Steak and Lobster Tail

Rating: Moderate   Time: 45 minutes

Suggested Wines: A dry red such as cabernet sauvignon or pinot noir

Ingredients:

Two 5-6 oz lobster tails	Salt and pepper
2 NY Strip Steaks	⅓ cup dry red wine
Butter	3 scallions, chopped
Olive oil	1 tbsp chopped parsley

Directions:

Simmer the lobster tails in a small pot of salted water for 12 minutes. Remove them from the pot to a plate to cool. While the lobster is cooking preheat a non-stick medium skillet or grill pan on medium heat and add 2 tbsp butter and 1 tbsp olive oil. Season the steaks with salt and pepper on both sides. Add the 2 steaks to the skillet when the pan is hot but not smoking. Brown on one side for 4-5 minutes and flip and brown on the other side for another 4-5 minutes, for medium rare and a couple minutes longer for medium (depending on the thickness of the meat and the temperature of the skillet).

Remove the steaks to a plate to rest and cover with aluminum foil, add a pat of butter on top of each filet. Reduce the heat to medium low and deglaze the skillet with the wine (remove the pan from the burner before adding the wine to prevent a fire) and also add the scallions. Season the sauce with salt and plenty of fresh cracked pepper. Simmer and reduce the wine by 50% and scrape the bits of meat off of the bottom of the skillet.

Melt 4 tbsp of butter in the microwave in a small bowl. Cut the lobster tails in half with a large chef knife on the underside so that the lobster meat is easily removed when dining. Arrange the lobster tails on two dinner plates and drizzle the melted butter over the lobster meat, season with a little pepper. Then transfer the filets to the plates and spoon about 1 tbsp of red wine reduction sauce over each filet.   Sprinkle a little parsley over the steaks and enjoy.

Steak Pocket Pies

Rating: Challenging   Time: 60 minutes

Suggested beverages: A cold micro brew beer or if you prefer wine, both dry whites or reds work well

Ingredients:

Puff pastry dough, one sheet
½ lb sirloin or strip steak cut into bite size cubes, fat removed

2 strips of bacon — Salt and pepper
1-2 tbsp dry rub — ⅓ cup dry red wine
1 medium onion, diced — ¼ tsp cumin
1 medium carrot, diced — ½ tbsp Worstershire sauce
6 cremini mushrooms, sliced — Olive oil
¼ red bell pepper, diced — Parchment paper
½ celery stalk, diced
Optional: ½ cup shredded cheddar cheese

Sauce:

½ cup half and half — Salt and pepper to taste
1 scallion, chopped — 1 pinch of cumin

Directions:

Sprinkle a little flour on a cutting board or on wax paper and the lay one piece of puff pastry dough on the flour. Roll the puff pastry to about ¼ inch thickness. Then cut two large rounds of dough, about 8-9 inches in diameter. Use a dish, paper plate or bowl to trace the circle with a paring knife.

Pre- heat the oven to 375 degrees. Heat a medium non-stick frying pan and fry the bacon. Remove the crisp bacon to paper towels and dice when cooled. Season the steak with a dry rub and brown in the bacon fat, add a little olive oil, on medium high. Stir fry the steak for about 4-5 minutes or until cooked to medium rare and remove from the heat and set aside to cool in a bowl. Then add all the veggies to the frying pan adding more oil if you need to and sauté for 5 minutes trying not to brown them. Season with salt and pepper. Spoon the veggies into the bowl with the steak to cool.

Remove the pan from the burner and add the wine, return to the burner and deglaze the pan by scrapping the bottom of the pan with a spatula and add the cumin and Worstershire sauce.

Put the bowl of meat and veggies in the refrigerator to cool. Once the steak has cooled spoon it into the center of the dough rounds with a slotted spoon. Add the cheese now. Fold the dough in half to make a pocket or half moon. Crimp the edges with a wet fork (dip the fork in water after each crimp). Brush a little olive oil on the top of each meat pie and place on a baking pan lined with parchment paper. Bake for about 20-25 minutes or until the crust is golden brown. Remove the pan from the oven and let cool. While it is cooling now make the sauce. Heat the frying pan on medium heat and add the sauce ingredients and stir constantly. Simmer for a few minutes and then transfer the pockets to plates and spoon a little bit of the sauce over top of each pocket and enjoy.

Lamb or Veal Shanks with Orzo Pasta
Rating: Moderate   Time: 3-4 Hours
Suggested Wines: Dry reds such as Burgundy or pinot noir
Ingredients:

2-4 lamb or veal shanks	2 bay leaves
16 oz beef stock, low sodium	½ tsp dried thyme
1 cup dry red wine	½ tsp dried rosemary
5 cloves garlic, crushed	4-6 oz orzo or ditalini pasta
1 medium yellow onion, diced	Salt and pepper
1 celery stalk, chopped	1 tbsp parsley, chopped
1 large carrot, chopped	

Directions:

In a large stock pot heat 2 tbsp of oil on medium heat. When hot add the meat to the pot and brown on each side for a minute or two. Remove the meat to a plate and add the onion, carrot and celery and sauté for 5 minutes, trying not to brown them. Reduce heat to medium low. Add the garlic for 30 seconds before adding the wine to deglaze the pot, scrapping the bottom with a wooden spoon (remove pan from stove when adding the wine). Let the wine simmer for a couple of minutes before adding the bay leaves and the meat. Add enough beef stock to cover the shanks. Season with salt and pepper to taste.

If the shanks are not fully submerged add stock or water to cover them. Partially cover the pot with a lid and simmer for 3 hours. Remove the cover at that time and increase the heat and simmer well to reduce the sauce. After another 30 minutes fill a small sauce pan (75% full) with the stock pot sauce and add the orzo and boil the orzo until tender, stirring frequently. Taste the sauce and re-season to your liking. When the orzo is tender spoon some out, with a slotted spoon into a pasta bowl or dinner plate. Transfer a lamb shank on top of the orzo, spooning on some additional sauce to your liking. Sprinkle with parsley and serve.

Lamb Braised with Olives and Wine

Rating: Moderate   Time: 60 minutes

Wine Recommendations: Bold red wine like a Chianti, Burgundy or pinot noir

Ingredients:

Small leg of lamb deboned & the fat trimmed, silver skin removed and cut into bite size cubes

4 cloves garlic, chopped	Olive oil
3-4 tbsp red wine vinegar	Salt
1 cup red wine	Red pepper flakes
20 green olives, pitted	2 tbsp parsley, chopped

Directions:

Heat olive oil in a deep skillet and add the lamb when the oil is hot but not smoking, on medium heat. Brown the lamb for 3-4 minutes turning a couple of times. Reduce the heat and add the garlic for ½ minute but don't let it burn, remove pan from stove and add the vinegar and the wine. Return pan to the stove and add the olives, salt and pepper to taste. Reduce heat and simmer lightly until the sauce is reduced by 50-75%. Add water if the lamb needs to cook longer so that there is some liquid in the pot. Spoon the meat and olives on a platter, sprinkle with parsley and serve. If you like you can check for doneness with a meat thermometer, lamb should be about 170 degrees.

Lamb Chops Grilled with Rosemary Wine Sauce

Rating: Moderate   Time: 30 Minutes

Suggested Wines: A hearty red wine such as a Bordeaux, Burgundy or zinfandel

Ingredients:

4 small lamb chops	2 cloves garlic, minced or crushed
Olive Oil	¾ cup of dry white wine
1 shallot, diced	Salt and pepper
½ tsp dried rosemary (or fresh)	Vegetable oil

Directions:

Pre-heat the outdoor grill for 20 minutes until the grill is hot (or use a grill pan on the stove). Brush a little vegetable oil on the gas or charcoal grill to help prevent sticking before you start it. While the grill is heating make the marinade. In a small sauce pan add 1 tbsp of olive oil and when warm add the shallot to soften, don't brown.   Sauté the shallot for 3-4 minutes and add the garlic and ½ tsp of rosemary for 30 seconds. Remove pan from stove and pour in the wine and a little salt and pepper. Return pan to stove and bring to a simmer for about 3 minutes or until the wine is reduced by half.

Then remove the sauce pan from the stove and bring to the grill with a brush. Season the chops on both sides with salt, pepper and a pinch of rosemary. Grill the chops on one side for about 3-4 minutes, brushing on the marinade several times during the grilling. Once one side has some good grill marks and a little charring, flip and grill the other side for about 3-4 minutes for medium rare. Brush with the marinade again. Remove the chops from the grill and rest, cover loosely with aluminum foil for 5 minutes. Plate the chops and spoon some additional marinade (be sure to spoon some of the shallots and rosemary) on top of the chops and serve warm.

Lamb or Veal Chops with Red Wine Reduction Sauce & Blue Cheese

Rating: Moderate   Time: 30 Minutes
Suggested Wines: A hearty red wine such as a pinot noir or Burgundy
Ingredients:

4 small lamb chops (or 2 veal chops)	¼ cup blue cheese (crumbled)
½ to ¾ cup dry red wine	Olive oil
3 shallots, chopped	Salt and pepper
3-4 mushrooms, sliced	Fresh parsley
½ tsp dried rosemary	

Directions:

Pre-heat 2 tbsp olive oil in a medium grill pan or a non-stick frying pan on medium heat. Season the chops on both sides with salt, pepper and rosemary. Place the chops in the pan when the oil is hot. Sear one side for 3-4 minutes, flip and sear the other side for about 3-4 minutes for medium rare (veal will take 4-5 minutes a side). Remove from the pan to rest and cover loosely with aluminum foil. Add the shallots, mushrooms and 1 tbsp oil to the pan and sauté for about 4 minutes, being careful not to burn the shallots. Turn off burner and add the wine and a pinch of dried rosemary, turn on burner and deglaze the pan, scrapping the meat bits with a spatula off the bottom. Simmer the wine until it's reduce by about half. Plate the chops and spoon the sauce, mushrooms and shallots on top and then add some crumbled blue cheese on top of the sauce. Sprinkle with fresh parsley and serve.

Veal Osso Buco (easy)

Rating: Easy   Time: 4 hours

Suggested Wines: Dry red such an pinot noir, cabernet sauvignon or Chianti

Ingredients:

4 medium veal shanks   ½ cup of flour, salt seasoned
4 cloves garlic, chopped   Olive oil
1 medium onion, diced   Parmesan cheese
1 bottle of dry red wine   2 large yukon gold potatoes
Salt and pepper   ¼ cup half and half or cream
1 tbsp of red pepper flakes   2 tbsp butter
½ cup fresh chopped parsley

Directions:

About four to five hours before you intend to eat you should start cooking or braising the veal shanks. In a large stock pot or dutch oven add 3 tbsp of olive oil and heat on medium heat. Dust each veal shank with the seasoned flour on all sides. Once the oil is hot add the veal shanks to the stock pot. Let the shanks brown before turning with tongs. Add more oil if the meat absorbs all of the oil. Brown the meat for 3-4 minutes in total. Add the onions and garlic during the last minute of cooking and more oil. Once the veal shanks are browned add about ¾ of a bottle of wine until the veal is covered slightly (turn off the burner before adding the wine and then restarting the burner). Add some water to cover if necessary. Bring the wine to a boil, reduce heat and simmer. Add the red pepper flakes, 1 tsp of fresh parsley and 1 tsp of salt. Simmer for 3-4 hours or until the meat is falling off of the bone. Add more wine or water as needed to the pot to ensure that the veal shanks remain mostly covered with sauce. Partially cover the pot. During the last hour of simmering remove the pot lid and let the liquid reduce by half and add more wine or water sparingly. Taste the wine sauce and re-season with salt and pepper as needed.

During the last 40 minutes of cooking, skin the potatoes, cut in quarters and boil in salted water until tender. Drain the water from the pot and add the half and half and the butter. Smash the potatoes with a hand masher (don't mash it too much as you want some texture), taste and season with salt and pepper. On two dinner plates spoon the potatoes and then place the shanks on top of the potatoes with some sauce. Sprinkle with parsley, cheese and serve.

Veal Cutlets Sautéed with Mushrooms and Wine

Rating: Easy   Time: 30 Minutes

Suggested beverage: cabernet sauvignon

Ingredients:

12-16 oz. boneless veal cutlets   Salt and pepper to taste

8 white/brown mushrooms sliced   1 tbsp fresh parsley

½ onion, diced   Butter

Marsala or Madeira wine   Olive oil

2 garlic cloves, crushed

Directions:

Heat a medium large non stick skillet with 1 tbsp butter and 1 tbsp of oil on medium. When the butter melts add the mushrooms and onions and lower the heat so that they cook slowly, don't brown them. Season veal with salt and pepper. After 4-5 minutes push the vegetables to the side and add the veal to the middle of the pan and sauté for 3 minutes a side on medium heat. Add more oil/butter if the pan is dry. Add the garlic for 30 seconds and then remove the pan from the stove and add ½ cup of wine. Return the pan to the stove and simmer for about 3-4 minutes until the alcohol burns off. Sprinkle with parsley and serve with mashed potatoes or pasta.

Pork Baby Back Ribs (easy)

Rating: Easy   Time: 90 Minutes

Suggested beverage: a good dark or lager beer

Ingredients:

One package of baby back pork ribs

2 cups of good barbecue sauce, with some heat

2 bay leaves   1 tbsp pepper

1 tsp dried thyme   2 cups wood chips like mesquite

2 tbsp salt

Directions:

Soak the wood chips in a bowl of water for 30 minutes. Fill a large pot with water and add the ribs, salt, bay leaf, thyme and pepper. The water should not come closer than about 2 or 3 inches from the top of the pot and the ribs should be covered with water. Bring the water to a simmer on medium high heat. Partially cover the pot with a lid and slow simmer for 1 hour. Test the ribs to see if they are tender, the meat should be pulling away from the bone. When you lift the ribs with tongs to a plate they may split into 2 sections, which is fine. Discard the cooking water.

Remove the wood chips from the water and wrap them in aluminum foil, leaving a small vent hole on top. Turn on the gas grill and place the wood ships in the foil directly on one of the outside burners. Heat the gas grill for 20 minutes or the charcoal grill until the coals are red hot. (You can also broil the ribs in the oven but without the wood chips, on the second rack from the broiler elements).

Once the wood chips start to smoke pretty well you can set the ribs on the grill and reduce the heat to medium and cover the grill. Flip the ribs after 5 minutes and brush with barbecue sauce and close the lid. After 5 minutes flip again and brush with barbecue sauce and cover for 2-3 minutes. The meat is already cooked, the grilling adds a nice grill flavor with the charring. The ribs should have grill marks on all sides. Remove the ribs to a pan or plate and cover with aluminum foil for 5 minutes to rest, then serve with some additional BBQ sauce.

Pork Tenderloin with Balsamic Vinegar Glaze

Time: 30 minutes   Rating: Moderate

Suggested Wines: Reds like Chianti, zinfandel and pinot noir

Ingredients:

1 pork tenderloin, 1 lb	1 tsp of brown sugar
½ cup good balsamic vinegar	Salt and pepper
½ cup of water	1 tbsp olive oil

Directions:

In a small sauce pan add the water, brown sugar and balsamic vinegar and heat on medium until the mixture is simmering. Season with salt and pepper. Reduce the mixture by about ⅓ rd and turn off the burner. Heat olive oil in a medium non-stick skillet until hot, but not smoking. Season the tenderloin with salt and pepper on all sides and place in the skillet and sear on all sides. You want a little charring all around the pork.

Preheat oven to 350. Move the pork to an baking dish and scrapes off the meat bits from the skillet and add to the sauce OR leave the pork in the skillet if its oven safe. Pour half of the balsamic vinegar sauce over the pork. Bake the pork in the oven for 15 - 20 minutes and check for doneness with a thermometer (170 degrees). Depending on the size of the tenderloin you may need to bake longer. When done, slice the pork and pour the remaining balsamic vinegar over the slices and serve.

Pork Country Ribs Grilled with Garlic Honey Barbecue Sauce

Rating: Easy   Time: 30 minutes
Suggested beverages: A cold micro brew beer or if you prefer wine, both dry whites or reds work well
Ingredients:

1-½ lbs whole country ribs	½ tsp fresh cracked pepper
¾ cup honey	½ tsp onion flakes
1 tsp garlic powder	1 tsp fresh or dried parsley
½ tsp salt	

Directions:

Pre-heat the gas or charcoal grill for about 20 minutes or until the grill is hot. If your grill has a side gas burner you can make the barbeque sauce on the burner. In a small sauce pan add all the ingredients except the ribs. Heat the sauce to a low simmer, do not boil. Stir the sauce thoroughly to combine all of the flavors. Once it has simmered for 2-3 minutes cover the pot to keep it warm and remove from the burner..

If your butcher left the country ribs whole you need to separate the ribs from each other with a knife and cut them in lengths of about 6 inches. Country ribs have a fair amount of fat (unlike baby back ribs) so we like to grill them on medium high heat relatively quickly.

Grill the ribs until charred with grill marks on one side for about 4 minutes and then flip and char the other side for another 4 minutes, depending on the temperature of your grill. Once the ribs are grilled rare reduce the heat to low and brush on the honey sauce and close the cover for 3-4 minutes, then open the cover and flip them and brush with more honey and cover for a couple of minutes. This added grilling time will bring the ribs to medium rare. Test the temperature with a thermometer (170 degrees). Pour any leftover honey sauce on a serving plate and with tongs lay the ribs on top of the honey and serve to your partner. Enjoy.

Pork Tenderloin Grilled with Homemade Barbeque Sauce

Rating: Easy   Time: 30 Minutes

Suggested Wines: We suggest a crisp chilled white wine or sparkling wine

Ingredients:

1 small pork tenderloin (about 1 lb)   Garlic powder

Salt and pepper

Barbeque sauce:

1 cup ketchup   1 tsp salt

¼ cup water   1 tsp fresh cracked black pepper

3-4 tbsp balsamic vinegar   1 tsp garlic powder

3-4 tbsp brown sugar   Optional: ½-1 tsp hot sauce

Directions:

   Add all of the barbeque sauce ingredients to a sauce pan and heat on medium until the sauce starts to simmer for 2-3 minutes and whisk it to combine all the flavors and turn off the heat. Let cool with the cover off the pan as some evaporation will help to concentrate the flavors. Taste the sauce and re-season to your liking.

   Preheat the gas or charcoal grill for 20 minutes or until the grate is hot. Season the pork tenderloin with salt, pepper and garlic powder. Clean the grates well and then place the tenderloin on the grill. Sear one side for about 2 minutes and turn and sear the other side for another couple of minutes until you get good grill marks on the meat. Brush a little barbeque sauce on the pork and then reduce the heat to medium or medium high and cover the grill. Let it roast on the grill for about 7-8 minutes and then turn it with tongs and brush again with barbeque sauce, lightly. Check for doneness after another 7-8 minutes with a thermometer (170 degrees). Avoid cutting open the pork as this allows the juices to escape. When it's nearly done brush more sauce on the pork and cover the grill again. Remove the cooked pork to a serving dish with tongs and pour the remaining sauce over the top of the pork. Let the pork rest for about 10 minutes (covered loosely with aluminum foil) before cutting as this helps to keep it juicy.

Pork and Rice Hawaiian Island Style

Rating: Moderate   Time: 45 minutes
Suggested Wines: A dry or semi sweet white wine goes well with this dish or a fruity martini or rum cocktail
Ingredients:

2 small boneless pork loin chops (6 oz each)
1 whole pineapple (or 8 oz canned)   White rice
¾ cup coconut milk (unsweetened)   Olive oil
½ cup shredded coconut   Salt and pepper

Directions:

Fresh Pineapple: Select a ripe pineapple from your grocer. It should be a little soft if squeezed on the bottom and you should be able to smell pineapple. Cut the pineapple in half length-wise and scoop out the inside of each half by using a sharp knife to cut between the fruit and the pineapple skin and then cutting lines from the top down to the skin in a crisscross pattern, but don't pierce the skin. The pineapple shell is going to be your serving dish, how cool is that !!

Pork: Pan fry the pork in olive oil for about 5 minutes per side, or until done to medium. Let the pork cool, season with salt and pepper and cut up into bite sized cubes.

Rice: In a large pot with a cover cook enough rice for 4 servings according to the directions on the package. When the rice is done add the coconut milk and shredded coconut to the pan and reduce the heat to low and stir. Add about a cup of diced fresh pineapple to the rice along with the diced pork. Stir the rice to combine and taste for seasoning with salt and pepper. Continue to stir the rice mix gently until it's warmed through and then spoon it onto each of the pineapple shells for serving or on dinner plates.

Baby Back Ribs (moderate)

Rating: Moderate   Time: 60 minutes
Suggested Wines: A great beer
Ingredients:

1 baby back rib (silver skin removed)
1 cup apple or pineapple juice   Dry rub
Aluminum foil   BBQ sauce (your favorite)

Sprig of rosemary (optional)

Directions:

Preheat gas or charcoal grill until the grill is hot, clean grill. Dry rub the ribs liberally and place the ribs on the grill. Grill them long enough to get grill marks on the ribs, about 3-4 minutes a side. Remove the ribs from the grill and wrap in aluminum foil. Open the top of the foil and pour in the juice and add the rosemary sprig, double wrap with more foil so it doesn't leak, crimp tightly and return to the grill, seam side up. Reduce the heat to low or 300 degrees, cover the grill and cook for 2 hrs and test for doneness. The ribs will be done when a rib bone easily pulls away from the meat. Remove the ribs from the foil and place them on the grill and brush with BBQ sauce, grill for 3-4 minutes and flip, brush again with BBQ sauce and grill for 3-4 minutes and serve.

Grilled Pork Chops with Peanut Butter and Honey Glaze

Rating: Moderate   Time: 30 minutes

Suggested Wines: A semi dry or dry white wine works equally well with this dish such as soave or pinot grigio

Ingredients:

2 large thick loin pork chops, center cut without bone (about 2 inches thick)

2-3 tbsp dry roasted salted peanuts, chopped

Salt and pepper   Honey

½ cup peanut butter

Directions:

Preheat the gas or charcoal grill for 20 minutes or until the grill is hot. Season the chops with salt and pepper on both sides. Lay the chops on the grill and char on both sides, about 2 minutes a side. After both sides are charred close the cover and reduce the heat to medium. Spoon the peanut butter and ¼ tsp of water into a cup and microwave for 30-60 seconds or until the peanut butter is a little watery. Flip the chops again after 4 minutes and continue cooking until done, perhaps another 4 minutes depending on how hot your grill is and how thick the chops are. When the pork is nearly done (170 degrees would be medium) spoon the peanut butter on top. Plate the pork chops and drizzle a little more honey and the chopped nuts over the top just before serving.

Lasagna with Meat Sauce (Bolognese)

Rating: Moderate   Time: 90 minutes

Suggested Wines: Bold red wine like a Chianti, Burgundy or pinot noir

Ingredients:

½ lb ground meatloaf mix

28 oz crushed tomatoes

2-3 garlic cloves, crushed

½ medium onion, minced

1 tbsp olive oil

½ lb lasagna noodles

½ lb ricotta cheese

8 oz mozzarella cheese

⅓ cup parmesan cheese

1 large egg, lightly beaten

½ tbsp of sugar

1 tbsp fresh parsley, chopped

½ tsp nutmeg

Salt and pepper

½ tbsp dried basil

Directions:

Boil the noodles according to the package directions, al dente or use "no-boil" lasagna. While the noodles are boiling, brown the ground meat and onion in a large skillet on medium heat with the oil. When the meat is cooked drain the excess fat from the pan and reduce the heat and then add the garlic for 1 minute and then add the tomatoes, basil and salt and pepper to taste. Simmer the meat sauce or bolognese sauce for 15-20 minutes and taste for seasoning. Remove the skillet from the stove.

In a mixing bowl add all of the ricotta, half of the mozzarella, egg, nutmeg, parsley, sugar and the parmesan cheese and mix well. Preheat oven to 375 degrees. In a 6" x 10" (approx.) baking dish spread about 1 cup of meat sauce, so that the bottom is covered. Place a row of lasagna noodles over the meat sauce, cut the noodles to fit. Add another layer of meat sauce, a layer of cheese and then a layer of noodles. Repeat the layering. Be sure to save some meat sauce to top off the layer of noodles. Top with any remaining cheese mix.   Place the baking dish on top of a sheet pan, cover the lasagna with aluminum foil and bake for 45 minutes. Uncover the lasagna and sprinkle the remaining mozzarella cheese on top and bake for 5 minutes or more until the cheese is bubbly. Let the dish stand on a cooling rack for 15 – 20 minutes before cutting and serving.

Meatballs with Sour Cream over Rice

Rating: Moderate | Time: 40 minutes

Suggested Wines: Dry reds such as Burgundy and Rioja

Ingredients:

½ lb ground veal

½ lb ground pork

1 large egg

2 tbsp seasoned breadcrumbs

1 cup cooked rice (brown or white)

½ cup half and half

8 cremini mushrooms, sliced

½ cup sour cream

6 scallions, chopped

¼ tsp thyme

¼ tsp basil

½ tsp salt

¼ tsp pepper

Olive oil

Salt and pepper to taste

1 tbsp parsley, chopped

Directions:

In a mixing bowl add the breadcrumbs, egg, salt, pepper, thyme, basil and meat and mix together with your hands. Heat a medium non-stick skillet on medium heat with 2 tbsp of olive oil. Form the meat into small meatballs with your hands, smaller than the size of a golf ball (1-½ inch diameter). As you form them, place them in the hot oil to brown. Roll them over when they brown on one side trying to brown them all around. After they've browned remove them all from the pan to a plate and add the mushrooms and half the scallions, reducing the heat to medium low. Scrape the bottom of the pan with a spatula. Sauté the mushrooms and scallions for 5 minutes and then add the half and half, the sour cream and the meatballs. Bring to s slow simmer and taste and re-season to your liking. Spoon the cooked rice onto dinner plates and spoon the meatballs and sauce over the top, sprinkle with parsley, scallions and serve warm.

Pasta Salad with Salami and Provolone

Rating: Easy | Time: 30 minutes

Ingredients:

5-6 oz pasta, such as rotini or penne

2 thick slices of Genoa salami, 1 inch thick

1 thick slice provolone, 1 inch thick

8 baby carrots, cut in quarters lengthwise

Your favorite Italian salad dressing, about 8-10 oz.

Salt and pepper | ½ red onion, diced

1 small zucchini, diced   12 kalamata olives, pitted

Directions:

   You will need to ask the deli attendant at your grocer to cut the salami and provolone extra thick. Dice the meat and cheese into ½ inch cubes. Boil the pasta according to the package directions and then drain the pasta and transfer it to a mixing bowl and sprinkle thoroughly with Italian dressing, stir and let cool, this keeps the pasta from sticking together. Add all of the other ingredients. Add more salad dressing, about ¼ of a cup to the pasta. Chill the pasta salad in the refrigerator, covered with plastic wrap.   The pasta will absorb a lot of the dressing in the refrigerator, so you will generally need to add more after chilling. Taste the pasta and add more dressing based on your preference. Season with salt and pepper to taste. Serve cold. You can substitute other meats like turkey, capicole or pepperoni, if you like.   Sometimes I add cooked shrimp instead of meat.

Meatless Entrées

Capellini with Pesto Sauce

Rating: Easy   Time: 20 minutes

Suggested Wines: Pinot grigio or soave

Ingredients:

⅓ lb capellini pasta

4 cloves of whole garlic

1 fresh basil, 10-15 leaves

2 tbsp Parmesan cheese

1 tbsp pine nuts

1 tsp salt and ½ tsp pepper

½ cup olive oil

Directions:

   Start boiling salted water in a large stock pot for the capellini but don't boil the pasta until everything else is ready as capellini only takes a couple of minutes to cook.

   Add the garlic, basil, parmesan cheese, pine nuts, salt and pepper to a blender or mini food processor. Pulse the blender once or twice to roughly chop the contents. Then turn the blender on medium speed and slowly pour the olive oil through the top opening in the blender until it forms a paste. Taste the pesto and re-season to your liking and pulse a few times. Cook the capellini according to the package instructions al dente and stir it several times to prevent sticking. Strain it and transfer the pasta to a large pasta bowl or platter and mix well with the pesto sauce. Sprinkle the top with parmesan cheese liberally and serve hot.

Gnocchi with Balsamic Sauce

Rating: Easy   Time: 30 minutes

Suggested Wines: Dry reds such as Burgundy or Chianti

Ingredients:

¾ cup imported balsamic vinegar

2 tbsp olive oil

1 package (12-16 oz) gnocchi

Salt and pepper to taste

2 scallions, chopped

Directions:

In a small sauce pan add the balsamic vinegar and olive oil and heat to a simmer, season with salt and pepper. Simmer for 10 – 15 minutes or until the sauce has reduced by about 25%. This concentrates the flavors. You should have about 1/2 of cup of sauce remaining. Turn off the heat and cover, leaving the pot on the stove. Cook the gnocchi according to the directions on the package. Strain it and divide between 2 pasta bowls or plates. Spoon the warm balsamic sauce over the top and then sprinkle both with chopped scallions. Be sure you serve this dish warm.

Macaroni and Cheese

Rating: Easy   <u>Time:</u> 45 minutes
Suggested Beverage: Chilled white wines such as chardonnay or cold beer
Ingredients:
2 cups grated sharp cheddar cheese
½ lb of uncooked elbow macaroni   ½ cup half and half
½ tsp salt and ¼ tsp pepper   Butter
Directions:

Preheat the oven to 375 degrees. Cook the pasta about 75% done, a little under-cooked and drain in a colander. While the macaroni is boiling butter the bottom and sides of a casserole dish and prepare the cheese.

Add 1-½ cups of cheese and the half and half in a mixing bowl (reserve ½ cup cheese). Season with salt and pepper. Add the pasta to the casserole bowl and pour the cheese mix on top. Stir the contents and taste and re-season if necessary. Bake uncovered for 20 minutes or until the macaroni mixture starts to bubble (you may wish to put a sheet pan under the casserole to keep your oven clean). Remove the casserole from the oven and turn the oven to broil – high. Sprinkle the remaining cheese on top of the macaroni. Broil in the oven until the cheese begins to brown and bubble watching it closely to prevent burning.

Linguini with Sautéed Onions and Capers

Rating: Easy   <u>Time:</u> 30 minutes
Wine Suggestions: Both a red or dry white wine will work with this dish
Ingredients:
¾ cup pinot grigio or other dry white wine or water

74

2 yellow onions, quartered, sliced thin
Optional: ¼ cup chopped roasted red peppers

⅓ lb dried linguini or spaghetti   Salt

3-4 cloves garlic, chopped   Olive oil

1 tbsp capers, without the juice   Parmesan cheese

1 tsp red pepper flakes

Directions:

Boil salted water in a stock pot for the pasta. Heat a large non-stick skillet on medium with 2 tbsp oil. When the oil is slightly hot in the skillet add the onions and sauté to caramelize, trying not to brown the onions. Sauté for 7-8 minutes or until they are tender and sweet. Add the garlic and sauté lightly for 30 seconds, do not brown the garlic. Remove the pan from the burner and add the wine and return to burner. Add red pepper flakes to the skillet and bring to a simmer.

Start boiling the pasta according to the directions on the package. Season the wine sauce with salt to taste. Once the sauce has simmered for about 4 minutes add the capers and roasted red peppers and reduce the heat to medium low and wait for the pasta to cook al dente. Drain the pasta in a colander and then pour it in with the sauce and onions, right in the skillet if there is room and heat for 1-2 minutes, stirring well with tongs. Scoop some pasta and sauce into pasta bowls, sprinkle with cheese and serve hot.

Risotto with Vegetables

Rating: Moderate   Time: 60 minutes

Wine Suggestions: chardonnay or pinot grigio

Ingredients:

1-½ cups Arborio rice   4 cloves garlic, chopped

12 mushrooms, sliced   1 medium onion, diced

2 cups diced zucchini or squash   3-4 tbsp olive oil

16 oz vegetable stock   Salt and pepper to taste

Water   1 tsp dried basil

Directions:

Heat the stock in a sauce pan but don't boil. Warm olive oil in a large skillet and sauté the onions and mushrooms on medium low until softened (about 5 minutes) being careful not to brown the onions. Add more oil as needed. Add the garlic for about a minute being careful not to burn it. Then ladle in a cup of broth and the rice into the skillet. Add more stock so that the skillet never gets dry and stir the rice frequently. Add water to the stock pot if you use up the broth. The rice should not stick to the pan, if it does then lower the temperature and add more stock. Continue stirring the rice until it's softened (about 20 minutes) and then add the zucchini, squash and the seasoning and cook for a couple of minutes. Taste the rice to make sure it's done, al dente, and serve.

Side Dishes

Baked Beans Italian Style

Rating: Moderate   Time: 30-40 minutes

Ingredients:

2 medium cans cannelloni beans (about 32 oz in total)

4 slices pancetta, diced   3-4 cloves of garlic, crushed

14-16 oz diced tomatoes   ½ medium onion, diced

½ cup of water   Salt

Olive oil   ¼ tsp red pepper flakes

¼ tsp dried sage   Parmesan cheese

¼ tsp dried basil   Option: 4 fresh basil leaves

Directions:

Heat 1 tbsp of olive oil in a medium large pot on medium heat. Once the oil is warm add the pancetta (or use bacon). Stir the pancetta until it's crispy. Add the onions and garlic and stir for 1 minute. Be careful not to burn the garlic.   Add the cannelloni beans, tomatoes and water to the pot and bring the mix to a simmer. Add more water during the cooking process as needed. Some liquid should remain in the pot or the beans will burn. Add the sage, red pepper flakes and basil to the pot and add salt to taste. Continue to simmer for about 20-30 minutes in total or until the beans start to break open. There should be a little liquid in the pot when you are done cooking, the sauce will thicken as it cools. Taste the baked beans and re-season with salt and pepper if needed. Spoon the Italian baked beans into a casserole dish or serving bowl, sprinkle with a little extra virgin olive oil and the fresh basil either whole or chopped and cover. Sprinkle with parmesan cheese just before serving.

Brussel Sprouts with Maple Syrup

Rating: Easy   Time: 15 minutes

Ingredients:

12-18 fresh brussel sprouts   2 tbsp real maple syrup

Salt and pepper   1 tbsp butter

Directions:

    Wash the sprouts and remove the outer layer of leaves. With a paring knife cut an X in the bottom of each sprout, near the stem. The cut should not be very deep. This cut helps to cook the inside of the sprout. In a small sauce pan bring about 2-3 inches of salted water to a boil on medium high heat. When the water boils add the sprouts, cover and reduce the heat to medium low and simmer for 5 minutes. After 5 minutes turn off the heat and pour the water out of the pot and add the butter and season with salt and pepper. There should be enough residual heat in the pot to melt the butter, but you may need to cover the pot with a lid for a minute or two. Gently swirl the pot to spread the butter over all of the sprouts. Then add the maple syrup and then gently swirl again to spread the syrup onto each sprout. Cover the pot until you're ready to serve.

Coleslaw with Horseradish

Rating: Easy   Time: 10 minutes

Ingredients:

16 oz precut packaged coleslaw mix

Salt and pepper   1 tbsp of white wine vinegar

1 tbsp prepared horse radish   Mayonnaise to taste

Directions:

    Wash and dry off the coleslaw mix and transfer to a bowl. Add 3-5 tbsp of mayonnaise to the bowl and stir. Add more mayonnaise as needed so that all of the cabbage is a little coated and season with salt and pepper to taste. Add the horseradish and vinegar and taste the coleslaw, adding more ingredients to your liking. Cover and refrigerate. Making this coleslaw several hours ahead of time will allow the flavors to develop.

Green Beans with Tomatoes and Bacon

Rating: Easy   Time: 15 minutes

Ingredients:

½ lb fresh green beans, cut in 2-3 inch lengths

1 cup chopped tomatoes   Salt and pepper

½ medium yellow onion, sliced   Olive oil

2 slices bacon, diced

Directions:

Heat 1 tbsp of olive oil to a non-stick medium frying pan and add the bacon when the oil is hot. Stir fry the bacon until brown and then add the onion and sauté for a couple of minutes. Then add the beans and tomatoes with the juices. Stir and sauté until the beans are tender. Add a little water to the pan if it goes dry. Taste and season with salt and pepper. Serve hot and enjoy.

Potatoes Mashed with Creamy Mushroom Sauce

Rating: Moderate   Time: 40 minutes

Ingredients:

2 large yukon gold or russet potatoes, peeled and boiled to tender

1 cup half and half   Butter

1 cup sliced white mushrooms   1 tbsp chopped fresh parsley

¼ tsp red pepper flakes   1 tbsp corn starch or flour

Salt and pepper

Directions:

Boil the potatoes and keep warm in the pot covered, drain the water. In a small sauce pan add 1-2 tbsp of butter and sauté the mushrooms for 8-10 minutes on medium. Add half and half and the red pepper flakes and bring the sauce to a simmer and reduce the sauce by about 50%. In a small cup, combine corn starch and ½ cup of water and stir well with a fork until the corn starch is fully dissolved, add this thickener to the sauce and bring to a slow boil, stirring constantly. Once the sauce has thickened turn off the burner and season with salt and pepper and add 1 tbsp of butter. Beat the boiled potatoes with an electric mixer, adding 1 tbsp butter, 1 tbsp half and half, salt and pepper to taste. Add a little more half and half if the mixture is too thick. Taste and re-season. Scoop the mashed potatoes into a serving bowl and top with the mushroom sauce and sprinkle with parsley and serve warm.

Potato Chips – Broiled and Healthy

This recipe is a healthy change from fried potatoes

Rating: Easy   Time: 30 minutes

Suggestions: These chips go well with grilled steaks, salmon or just as a snack

Ingredients:

2 or 3 large white potatoes (or red)   Salt and pepper

Vegetable oil or cooking spray   Ketchup
Directions:

Leave the skin on the potatoes and slice them very thin with a mandolin, food processor or a knife. The chips should be round. Very lightly grease a sheet pan with vegetable oil. Lay the chips on the pan flat and season the top side with salt. Broil them in your oven about 2 inches from the broiler element on high heat. You will need to watch them carefully to ensure they don't burn. Once the tops of the chips are golden brown and maybe have a little charring remove the pan from the oven and turn the chips over to broil the other side. Salt the second side after you turn the chips. Return the pan to the oven and broil until the tops are golden brown. When done transfer them to a plate and season with salt and pepper and serve. The chips get soggy pretty quickly, so serve soon after broiling, with ketchup if you like.

Spinach, Creamy with Parmesan Cheese

Rating: Easy   Time: 20 minutes
Ingredients:
16 oz baby spinach leaves   Salt and pepper
½ cup cream or half and half   Butter
3 cloves garlic, crushed   1 tbsp parmesan cheese
2 tbsp onions, finely diced
Thickener: 1 tbsp corn starch or flour dissolved and stirred vigorously in ½ cup of water in a small glass
Directions:

In a medium large non-stick skillet heat 2 tbsp of butter on medium heat. When the butter starts to melt add the onions and sauté for 3-4 minutes being careful not to burn the butter. Add the garlic and sauté for another minute, add more butter if necessary. Then add the cream and parmesan cheese, season with salt and pepper and bring to a slow simmer. Let it simmer for about 3 minutes. Pour the thickener into the skillet and bring to a simmer again, stirring constantly with a wooden spoon or whisk. Taste the sauce and re-season to your liking. As soon as the sauce has thicken add the spinach and mix the spinach into the cream sauce for about 1 minute, just enough to wilt the spinach a little. Transfer the spinach to a serving bowl, pour all the sauce remaining in the pan on top of the spinach and add a pat of butter and serve warm.

Red Potato Salad

Rating: Easy   Time: 30 minutes

Ingredients:

6 medium red potatoes   Italian dressing

15-20 fresh green beans   Salt and pepper

6 large radishes sliced thin

Directions:

    Cut the potatoes in quarters and place them in a stock pot. Cover the potatoes with salted water and bring to a boil. Trim the stem end off the washed green beans but don't cut them any further. When the potatoes are tender add the green beans, reduce the heat and simmer for 5 more minutes. Drain the beans and potatoes thoroughly in a colander. Once you are satisfied that all excess water has been eliminated transfer the potatoes and beans to a serving bowl and sprinkle on the Italian dressing to your taste. Spread the radishes on top, season liberally with fresh cracked pepper and stir. Cover the bowl and refrigerate for half an hour or more. After the potatoes have chilled taste the potatoes and green beans, re-season with salt and pepper and add more dressing according to your personal tastes. You can also serve this warm if you prefer by skipping the refrigeration.

Spaghetti Squash Sautéed with Garlic and Olive Oil

Rating: Moderate   Time: 45 minutes

Ingredients:

1 small spaghetti squash cut in half, length wise

2-3 tbsp olive oil   Parmesan cheese

4 cloves garlic, crushed   Fresh parsley

Salt and pepper

Directions:

    With the skin side down, steam the squash with a steamer basket for about 30 minutes in a large covered stock pot with water. You will know the squash is done when you can scrape strands of squash off with a fork. Remove the squash from the pot and let it cool down. Once it has cooled, scrape all the squash off of the skin with a fork into a mixing bowl. In a large skillet or pot heat the oil over medium heat. When the oil is hot pour in the spaghetti squash and season with salt and pepper. Heat the squash through, for 5 minutes stirring constantly with tongs. Spoon the squash to the sides of the pan and add the garlic to the bottom of the pan into some olive oil and sauté for about 60 seconds. If it starts to brown remove the skillet from the heat. Pour the squash into a serving bowl and taste for salt and pepper and re-season. Sprinkle it with parmesan cheese and parsley liberally and serve.

Apples Baked with Turnips

Rating: Moderate   Time: 30 minutes
Ingredients:
2 medium turnips peeled and cut into 1 inch square pieces
2 Macintosh apples peeled, cored, cut into wedges or slices
Salt and pepper   Butter
Directions:

    In a medium sauce pan bring about 3-4 inches of water to a boil and then add the turnips and boil for 3-4 minutes covered. Then add the apples and season with salt and pepper and reduce the heat to a simmer. Once the turnips and apples are soft turn off the heat and drain out the water. Lightly mash the apples and turnips with a potato masher, but leave the consistency chunky. Season with salt and pepper to your taste. Transfer the turnips and apples to a casserole dish, cover and warm the dish in the oven for 10 minutes at 225 degrees. Remove from the oven add a couple of pats of butter and serve.

Greens Sautéed with Garlic and Olive Oil

Rating: Easy   Time: 10 minutes
Ingredients:
1 bunch of greens such as spinach or swiss chard
1-2 tbsp olive oil   Salt and pepper to taste
4 cloves crushed garlic
Directions:

    Trim the stems from the greens and remove any brown leaves. Wash and thoroughly dry the greens with paper towels. Heat a medium skillet with olive oil on medium heat. When the oil is hot but not smoking add the greens and season with salt and pepper. Turn the spinach with tongs constantly for about 1 minute and taste, if the spinach is cooked to your liking reduce the heat and add the garlic and sauté for another minute and remove to a serving bowl.

For swiss chard, which takes longer to cook, sauté it in the oil for a couple of minutes and add the garlic and sauté for 1 minute more. Add ¼ cup of water and cover to steam the swiss card for a minute or two to complete the cooking. With tongs move the greens to a serving bowl and mix well so that the garlic is well spread in the greens. Taste and re-season to your liking.

Butternut Squash Roasted with Honey and Walnuts

Rating: Easy   Time: 1 hour and 15 minutes

Ingredients:

1 small butternut squash, cut in half lengthwise and seeds removed

½ cup chopped walnuts   2-3 tbsp butter

¼ cup half and half   Salt and pepper to taste

2 tbsp honey   Optional: 3 tbsp raisins

Directions:

Preheat the oven to 375 degrees. Season the squash with salt and pepper. Roast both halves of the butternut squash for 45-50 minutes with the skin side down in the roasting pan or sheet pan, layered with aluminum foil or baking paper. Test the squash for doneness by pricking the fattest area of the squash with a sharp knife. The knife should go in and back out easily with no resistance if done. Continue roasting until done. Remove the pan and let the squash cool. When cool, scoop the squash out of the skin and into a mixing bowl. Add the half and half, honey and butter. With an electric mixer beat the squash, with a slow setting for about a minute. The consistency should not be too smooth; you still want a little texture to the squash. Season with salt and pepper and taste and re-season. Transfer the squash to a casserole dish. Stir in the walnuts, raisins and cover the casserole dish and bake for 10-15 minutes at 350 degrees. After 10 minutes stir the squash and taste for seasoning. Add more honey, salt or pepper according to your tastes. Serve the squash warm with a little more butter on top.

Cauliflower Sautéed with Onions

Rating: Easy   Time: 10 minutes

Ingredients:

2 cups of fresh cauliflower   ½ medium yellow onion, sliced

Olive oil   Salt and pepper

Directions.

Cut flowerets off of a head of washed cauliflower and then cut the flowerets in half, about two cups worth. Heat a medium non stick skillet over medium heat with 2-3 tbsp of olive oil. When the olive oil is hot add the cauliflower (cut side down) and onions to the skillet and don't touch them, do not stir. Turn heat down to medium low. You want the vegetables to brown. This brings out the sugars in the cauliflower and onions. Add olive oil if the pan dries out. Season with salt and pepper. After a couple minutes lift one piece of cauliflower from the pan to see if it's golden brown. If it is, turn all of the pieces with tongs and brown on the other side. Once both sides are golden brown remove from heat and spoon the veggies onto plates. Taste and re-season before serving.

Carrots Baked with Horseradish

Rating: Easy   Time: 20 Minutes

Ingredients:

2 cups of mini fresh carrots   ½ cup of breadcrumbs

2-3 tbsp prepared horseradish   Salt and pepper

Directions:

Steam the carrots for 5 minutes in a pot with a steamer. Immediately transfer the carrots to a small casserole dish for baking. Preheat the oven to 350 degrees. Season the carrots with salt and pepper. In a mixing bowl combine the horseradish and bread crumbs and season with salt and pepper. Pour half of the breadcrumb mix over the carrots and stir to combine. Pour the remaining breadcrumb mix on top of the carrots and do not stir. Cover the casserole dish and bake in the preheated oven for 8-10 minutes, remove from the oven and let the carrots cool a few minutes before serving. Add more horseradish if you prefer if spicy.

Greens and Beans

Rating: Medium   Time: 20 Minutes

Ingredients:

12 oz of collards or swiss chard   ½ tsp red pepper flakes
16 oz canned cannelloni beans   ¼ cup dry white wine (or broth)
½ cup dried elbow macaroni   ¼ cup veggie broth or water
3 garlic cloves, chopped   Salt and pepper
Olive oil

Directions:

Pre-heat a small pot of salted water for the pasta. Clean the greens thoroughly and chop roughly and discard the stems. Drain the juice from the beans. Heat a medium skillet on medium heat and add 2 tbsp of olive oil. When the oil is hot add the greens to the pan and heat until they are slightly wilted stirring with tongs. Add the garlic for 30 seconds being careful not to burn it and then add the wine, water, beans and cover for about 10 minutes until the greens are tender and the beans are hot. Season with salt and pepper. Boil the pasta according to the directions on the package. Drain when done. Remove the cover of the greens pan and allow the liquid to reduce for a couple of minutes. Taste the greens and re-season to your liking. Once the sauce is reduced by 50%, add the cooked macaroni to the pan, stir and serve in a bowl with some of the wine sauce.

Corn on the Cob Grill Roasted

Rating: Easy   Time: 1 Hour

Ingredients:

2 fresh ears of corn

Directions:

Soak 2 ears of corn for 30-40 minutes in a bowl of water. Pre-heat your grill for 20 minutes on high and clean your grill. Remove the corn from the water and pull back the husk and remove the corn hair and return the husk leaves back into the original position. Reduce the heat to medium high and place the corn cobs on the warming rack and roast for 15-20 minutes. If your grill doesn't have a warming rack you can heat the two outside burners and leave the inside burners off and place the corn over the inside burners. The corn will be done when it's tender which you can test by pricking a kernel with a fork, the corn should be soft. It's okay to have a little charring on the corn. It may take a little practice to achieve perfect results on your grill but it will be worth the effort.

Sweet Potatoes Roasted and Creamy

Rating: Moderate   Time: 60-75 minutes

Ingredients:

2 large fresh sweet potatoes   Butter

Half and half or cream   Honey

Salt and pepper   1 tbsp parsley, chopped

Directions:

    Roast the sweet potatoes whole, skin on, in a roasting pan lined with aluminum foil at 400 degrees in the oven for about 45 minutes. Check for doneness by piercing the largest potato with a fork or sharp knife and see if the fork pulls easily out, when it does it's done.   Remove the potatoes to cool. After they cool you can now easily peel the potatoes with your hands and a small paring knife. Discard the skin. Cut the potatoes into quarters and toss into a large mixing bowl. Season with salt and pepper and add 1 tbsp butter and 3-4 tbsp of half and half and mix with an electric mixer on medium for 1 minute. The consistency of the sweet potatoes should be creamy, add more half and half if it's still a little lumpy or thick. Once you get it to your desired consistency add a couple of tbsp of honey, mix with the mixer for about 60 seconds and taste. Add more salt, pepper, butter or honey to get it the way you like it and re-mix. Transfer to a covered casserole dish and re-heat the sweet potatoes in your microwave oven for 3-4 minutes, stirring twice to distribute the heat. Sprinkle with parsley and a pat of butter and serve warm.

Kidney Beans Southwest Style

Rating: Easy   Time: 15 minutes

Suggestions: This side dish goes well with Mexican or Southwest dishes

Ingredients:

16 oz canned kidney beans, rinsed and drained

2 slices bacon or bacon flavored tempeh, diced

½ medium yellow onion, diced   2-3 tbsp jalapeno, chopped

¼ bell pepper, diced   3 garlic cloves, crushed

Directions:

In a medium non-stick skillet, fry the bacon until crisp in a little oil. Add the onion and peppers to the pan and sauté for 5 minutes, trying not to brown them, on medium low heat. Add the garlic and kidney beans to the pan, and after a minute add 2 tbsp of water and deglaze the bottom of the pan, scrapping with a spatula. Once the beans are hot remove from the heat and serve warm.

Red Cabbage and Apples Steamed With Honey

Rating: Easy   Time: 45 - 60 minutes

Ingredients:

16 oz bag of precut red cabbage or half of a head of a small red cabbage that you've sliced thin

1-2 large sweet apples peeled and sliced

3 tbsp honey   Salt and pepper to taste

1 tbsp red wine vinegar   Optional: a pinch caraway seeds

Directions:

Bring 2-3 inches of water to a simmer in a stock pot and add the vinegar, apple, red cabbage, caraway seeds, salt and pepper and cover the pot. Reduce the heat to medium and steam the cabbage for 30 minutes. Stir occasionally and add more water as needed so that there is 1 to 2 inches in the pot. Add the honey and steam for another 5 minutes and taste. The cabbage should be tender and a little sweet. Re-season to your liking. If the cabbage is not tender, continue to steam. Scoop the cabbage out with tongs into a serving dish, leaving the water in the pot. Pour a little bit of honey over the cabbage and serve hot.

Couscous

Rating: Easy   Time: 10 minutes

Ingredients:

¾ cup plain couscous   6 mushrooms, sliced

1 small onion, diced   2 cloves garlic, crushed

Directions:

Sauté veggies in olive oil for 2 minutes in a medium pot on low heat being careful not to burn the garlic. Add 1-½ cups of water to the pot and bring it to a boil. Add the couscous. Season with salt and pepper. Remove it from the burner and cover the pot for 5 minutes. Taste, re-season and serve.

Soups

Note: the soups can be made a day ahead of time if you like, refrigerated and reheated

Leak and Potato Creamy Soup
Rating: Moderate   Time: 45 minutes
Ingredients:
1 large white or russet potato, peeled and diced
3-4 large leaks   1 medium yellow onion, diced
1 stalk celery, chopped   Butter
3 cloves crushed garlic   Salt
16 oz veggie or chicken stock   ¼ tsp dried thyme
1 cup half and half   White or black pepper
2 tbsp olive oil   1 tbsp chopped fresh parsley
Directions:

Cut the leaks in half length-wise and immerse them in water in your sink to remove all sand particles. Dry the leaks and cut off the dark green ends and the root end and keep the lighter portion of the leaks and chop roughly. In a large sauce pot heat the oil and 1 tbsp of butter on medium and add the leaks, onion and celery as soon as the oil is hot. Sauté the leaks and celery for 5 minutes but avoid browning them. Add the garlic and sauté another minute. Add more butter or oil if your pan starts to run dry. Add the stock, thyme and potatoes and bring to a simmer. Simmer for 20 minutes or until the leaks and potatoes are tender. Add salt and pepper to taste. Turn off the heat and let the soup cool a little. Puree the soup in either a food processor or submersible blender. After blending, return the soup to the original pot for finishing. Add the half and half and simmer for 5 minutes and then add 2 tbsp of butter and stir until melted. Ladle into bowls and sprinkle with parsley. It's even better – reheated the next day.

Roasted Butternut Squash Soup

Rating: Moderate   Time: 1-1/2 hours

Ingredients:

1 medium butternut squash, cut length way in half and seeds removed

Salt and pepper to taste   1 cup veggie or chicken broth

1 cup of half and half   2 scallions, chopped

½ medium onion, diced   Olive oil

½ stalk of celery, chopped   Butter

1 medium carrots, chopped   Optional: sour cream

Directions:

Preheat oven to 375 degrees, place the butternut squash halves in a roasting pan lined with aluminum foil, skin side down and roast for 45 – 60 minutes in the oven. The squash will be done when you can pierce the center of the squash easily with a fork. Let the squash cool and then scoop out the pulp into a bowl from the squash skin and throw out the skin.

In a large pot sauté the onions, carrots and celery in 1-2 tbsp of olive oil and 1 tbsp of butter on medium heat for 5 minutes. You do not want to brown them, you just want to lightly sauté the onions, carrots and celery to extract the flavors. After 5 minutes add the broth and the squash. Stir the pot and season with salt and pepper to your taste. Bring the soup to a boil and simmer for 5 minutes and remove the pot from the burner. Puree the soup with a submersible blender or in a food processor. Return the pureed soup to the original pot and bring to a simmer on medium high heat. Once the soup starts to simmer add the half and half and reduce heat to medium and bring to a simmer slowly. Taste for seasoning and add salt and pepper as needed. Let the soup simmer slowly for 5 minutes, this will help to thicken it. Add 1 tbsp of butter and once melted turn off the heat and cover the pot.

When you're ready to serve the soup, ladle it into soup bowls and sprinkle the scallions on the top of the soup. Also, add a dollop of butter or sour cream (your choice) just before serving.

Baked Bean Soup

Rating: Moderate   Time: 60 minutes

Suggestions: Serve with warm crusty bread such as Italian or French

Ingredients:

32 oz canned cannelloni beans (or black beans)

32 oz chicken or veggie broth   2 tbsp red bell pepper, diced

1 large yellow onion, finely diced   Salt and pepper

4 oz bacon, diced   ½ tsp, dried thyme

2 tbsp olive oil   2 bay leaves

(optional - for a vegan soup substitute bacon flavored tofu for the bacon)

Directions:

In a stock pot heat the oil on medium heat and add the bacon when hot. Fry the bacon lightly for 2-3 minutes. Then add the onions for 5-6 minutes to soften them, but don't brown them. Add the broth, thyme and bay leaves and bring to a simmer. Rinse the cannelloni beans in a colander. When the pot simmers add the cannelloni beans to the soup. Season with salt and pepper and taste it. Simmer on low for about 50-60 minutes with the cover on the pot or until the beans break open and thicken the soup. Be sure to add a little water if it becomes too thick during simmering so that you don't burn the beans. Taste and re-season to your personal preference. Remove the bay leaves and ladle the hot soup into soup bowls. Sprinkle some diced red bell pepper on top and serve.

Creamy Cauliflower Soup

Rating: Moderate   Time: 45-60 minutes

Ingredients:

1 cauliflower with flowerets cut off   1 cup half and half or light cream

2 stalks celery, chopped   2 tbsp olive oil

1 medium yellow onion, diced   Butter

3 scallions, chopped   Salt and white/black pepper

¼ tsp dried thyme   ½ cup shredded sharp cheese

16 oz chicken or veggie broth

Directions:

In a medium stock pot heat the oil on medium and add the celery and onion when the oil is hot. Sauté the celery and onion gently, trying not to brown them. Cut the floweret's and stems into bite size pieces. Take one cup of flowerets and separate from the rest, as you will add these after the soup has been pureed.

After cooking the onions for 5 minutes add 2 tbsp of butter and the cauliflower. Stir the mix and sauté lightly for a couple of minutes. Then add the broth and bring to a simmer. Simmer the soup until the cauliflower is very soft and falling apart about 20 minutes. Season with thyme, salt and pepper. Stir and remove the pot from the burner. Puree the soup with a submersible blender or a food processor in batches. Blend until the soup is smooth. Return the pot of soup to the burner and bring it to a simmer on medium heat. Add the reserved cauliflower. Simmer for 5 minutes and add the half and half. Continue to simmer until the added cauliflower is tender. Taste and re-season to your personal tastes. Ladle into soup bowls and sprinkle with scallions and add a pat of butter and the cheese.

Meatball Soup

Rating: Moderate   Time: 45 Minutes

Ingredients:

¼ lb ground veal or meatloaf mix   ½ tsp garlic powder
¼ cup mini pasta like ditallini   2 tbsp parsley
½ celery stalk, diced finely   1 bay leaf
½ medium onion, diced finely   ½ tsp dried thyme
6-8 baby carrots cut into thin strips   1 cup spinach, chopped
2 garlic cloves, chopped   32 oz chicken or veggie broth
Salt and pepper to taste   Olive oil

(you can substitute little frozen meatballs from your grocer if you're rushed for time)

Directions:

Place the ground meat in a mixing bowl and season with salt, pepper and garlic powder. Form the ground meat into little meatballs about the circumference of a quarter, or less. Heat a soup pot on medium heat with 2 tbsp of olive oil. When the oil is hot add the little meatballs but don't crowd them, fry in batches. After one side has browned turn them and brown the other side. Don't worry if you break a couple. After frying, remove the meatballs to a dish and add the onions, carrots and celery to the pot, season with salt and pepper and sauté the veggies for about 5 minutes. Add more oil if the pot becomes a little dry. Add the garlic for 30 seconds being careful not to brown it. Then add the broth, spinach, thyme, half of the parsley, bay leaf, pasta and scrape the bottom of the pot to release the delicious bits into the soup. Season with salt and pepper. Add the meatballs back into the pot and cover and simmer lightly for about 15 minutes. Taste the soup and re-season with salt and pepper to your liking. Remove the bay leaf and serve hot. Sprinkle a little fresh parsley on top.

Chunky Chicken Soup with Farfalle Pasta

Rating: Moderate   Time: 1 Hour

Suggestions: This soup goes well with panini sandwiches or mini pizzas

Ingredients:

2-3 chicken thighs, skin removed   1 bay leaf
½ cup mini farfalle pasta   ¼ tsp dried thyme
1 celery stalk, diced   ¼ tsp celery seed
1 medium onion, diced   2 scallions, chopped
½ cup carrots, chopped   1 tbsp fresh parsley
¼ cup frozen corn   6 whole pepper corns
Salt and pepper to taste   1 tsp of parsley for garnish

Directions:

Simmer the whole chicken pieces in 6 cups of salted water and bay leaf for about 30 minutes in a covered pot. Remove the chicken to a plate to cool and discard the bay leaf. Pour the chicken broth through a strainer into a bowl and cool in the refrigerator uncovered, if a film of chicken fat solidifies on the top of the broth, spoon it off and discard.

Remove the chicken bones and gristle from the thighs and cut all of the chicken into good size cubes, about one inch square or larger. Return the chicken broth to the pot and add the vegetables, chicken and all other ingredients except the garnish, partially cover and bring to a simmer. Taste the soup and re-season with salt and pepper. Simmer for 20 minutes and then add the macaroni. Simmer until the macaroni is tender and turn off the burner so as not to overcook it. Taste the soup again and re-season, remove the bay leaf. Serve hot with a sprinkling of parsley.

Creamy Corn Soup with Ham

Rating: Easy   Time: 30 minutes

Important: Ask your deli to slice one piece of ham extra thick, about 1 inch thick

Ingredients:

1 slice of ham (1 inch thick), diced   ½ tsp cumin
1 can of creamed corn (16 oz)   ½ tsp chili powder
3 cloves garlic, crushed   ¼ tsp cayenne pepper
1 can chicken stock (16 oz)   ½ cup heavy cream/half and half
½ medium onion, diced   1 tsp chopped fresh parsley

Butter or olive oil   Salt
Directions:

In a large sauce pot melt 2 tbsp of butter on medium low heat. Add the onion and sauté for 4-5 minutes. Then add the garlic and sauté for another minute being careful not to burn it. Add the creamed corn, chicken stock, cumin, cayenne, chili powder and salt to taste. Bring to a simmer reduce heat to medium and add the cream and ham. Slowly simmer for 15 minute, adding in a tbsp of butter during the last minute. Taste and re-season to your liking and add the parsley.

Potato and Bacon Cream Soup
Rating: Moderate   Time: 60 minutes
Suggested Sides: Warm crusty Italian bread and a tossed salad
Ingredients:
3 large white potatoes, peeled & quartered
32 oz chicken or veggie broth   Butter
1 medium onion, diced   Salt and pepper to taste
1 celery stalk, chopped   ¼ tsp dried thyme
4 slices bacon, diced   1 scallion, chopped
½ cup half and half
Directions:

Heat a large pot on medium heat and add the bacon with a little butter. Crisp the bacon and remove the bacon to a paper towel to drain. Add the celery and onions to the pan and sauté on medium heat for 5 minutes, don't brown the onions, adding more butter if you need to. Pour the broth in the pot and scrape the bacon bits off of the bottom with a spatula. Add the thyme and the potatoes to the pot and bring to a slow boil. Boil for about 25 minutes and test the potatoes to see if they are done by piercing them with a fork. If the fork slides out easily then the potatoes are done.

When the potatoes are done, scoop out 3-4 tbsp of potatoes with a slotted spoon and put them in a bowl to cool a bit and then cut these reserved potatoes into 1 inch or smaller cubes. We will add these potato cubes back into the soup after we puree the soup. With a submersible blender puree the soup until it's smooth and creamy (or use a food processor). Add the bacon and the half and half and simmer for 10 minutes uncovered to reduce the soup, add the reserved potato cubes and simmer a couple of additional minutes and turn off the heat. Taste the soup and season with salt and pepper to your taste. Ladle the soup into 2 soup bowls and sprinkle with scallions.

Cream of Asparagus Soup

Rating: Moderate   Time: 45-60 minutes

Ingredients:

1 bunch of asparagus, woody stem ends removed
1 medium white potato, skinned and diced
1 stalk celery, chopped   1 cup half and half or cream
1 medium yellow onion, diced   2-3 tbsp olive oil
2 scallions chopped   Butter
1/4 tsp dried thyme   Salt and white/black pepper
16 oz chicken or veggie broth

Directions:

In a medium stock pot heat the oil on medium and add the celery and onion when the oil is hot. Sauté the celery and onion gently, trying not to brown them. Cut the flower tips off of the asparagus and set aside to add later. Cut the remaining stems into 1 inch pieces. After cooking the onions for 5 minutes add 2 tbsp of butter and the asparagus stems (don't add the tips yet) and the potato. Stir the mix and sauté lightly for a couple of minutes and add the broth and bring to a simmer. Simmer the soup until the asparagus and potato are very soft (about 20 minutes). Season with thyme, ½ tsp salt and ¼ tsp pepper. Stir and remove the pot from the burner. Puree the soup with a submersible blender or in a food processor in batches, until the soup is smooth. Return the pot of soup to the burner and bring to a simmer and add the reserved asparagus tips. Simmer for 5 minutes and add the half and half. Continue to simmer until the asparagus is tender. Taste and re-season to your liking. Ladle into soup bowls with chopped scallions and a pat of butter.

Salmon and Cheddar Cheese Cream Soup

Rating: Challenging   Time: 45 – 60 minutes

Ingredients:

½ lb fresh salmon fillet   ½ yellow med. onion, diced
3 cloves garlic, crushed   1 stalk celery, chopped

¼ tsp dried thyme
1 c. grated sharp cheddar cheese
32 oz chicken or veggie stock
1 bay leaf
1 cup half and half or cream

Salt and pepper
Olive oil
Butter
1 tbsp chopped fresh parsley

Directions:

In medium skillet on medium heat poach the salmon (skin side down) in 1-2 inches of salted water with a bay leaf. Simmer for 15-20 minutes, or until the inside of the salmon is cooked. Remove the salmon from the poaching liquid and let cool on a plate. Continue simmering the poaching liquid to reduce and concentrate the flavors. Remove the skin and discard. Save 2-3 tbsp of poaching liquid as it will have some nice flavor to the soup. Cut the salmon into quarters.

In a stock pot heat 1 tbsp of butter and 1 tbsp of olive oil on medium heat. Add the onions and celery and sauté them for about 3 minutes and add the garlic and sauté for another minute. Add the stock and heat to a simmer. Once it starts to simmer add the salmon, thyme and a couple of tbsp of the poaching liquid. Simmer for 15 minutes and then blend the soup with a submersible blender or in small batches in a food processor. The consistency of the soup should be smooth. Add the half and half to the soup and simmer for 5-10 minutes, uncovered. Taste the soup and season with salt and pepper. Add ¾ of the cheddar cheese and stir until the cheese melts completely. Ladle the soup into soup bowls and top the soup with the remaining cheddar cheese, parsley and serve.

Greens and Beans Soup

This is wonderful Italian soup which can be made vegetarian or add little meatballs and turn it into Italian wedding soup.

Rating: Easy   Time: 45 minutes

Ingredients:

12 oz greens – kale, spinach, swiss chard or collards
32 oz vegetable stock
3-4 cloves garlic, chopped
½ yellow onion, diced
1 stalk celery, chopped

¼ tsp dried thyme
¼ tsp dried oregano
Salt and pepper to taste
16 oz canned cannellini beans

2-3 tbsp olive oil

1 cup white wine, optional

1 tbsp chopped fresh parsley

Directions:

We recommend that you buy the freshest greens can you can find, so use kale if that's the freshest looking green. Wash the greens and tear the leaves from the stalks and discard the stalks. Chop leaves into bite size pieces, about an inch square.

In a stock pot heat the oil and sauté the onions and celery on medium low but don't brown them for 3-4 minutes. Add the garlic being careful not to brown it, for a minute. Add the wine away from the burner to deglaze the pan (or use water) and bring to a simmer for 2-3 minutes on medium high heat. Add the stock, greens and herbs and bring pot to a simmer. For spinach and swiss chard simmer for 5-10 minutes (which cook quickly) and for kale and collards simmer for 30 minutes or until tender. Add the beans and simmer on low for 15 minutes more, with the pot partially covered. Add water as the stock evaporates during cooking. Season with salt and pepper to your taste and serve or refrigerate for later, for up to a week.

Desserts

Baby Chocolate Cheesecakes

Rating: Moderate   Time: 30 minutes

Ingredients:

¼ cup of chocolate or raspberry syrup

4 oz of cream cheese at room temperature

Fresh raspberries, strawberries or blueberries

2 tsp of sugar   2-3 tbsp Oreo™ cookie crumbs

1 large egg   Cupcake foils

¼ tsp of vanilla extract

Directions:

    Smash the cookie crumbs to a fine consistency in a zip lock type bag to the size of grains of sand. In a cupcake pan place two cupcake foils. Spoon about a tbsp of the cookie crumbs into the bottom of each cupcake foil. In a bowl add the syrup, cream cheese, vanilla, sugar and egg and mix until fully incorporated with an electric mixer. Pour the mix into each cupcake – not quite to the top as the cheese cakes will rise. If you have leftover cheesecake you can make a third baby cheesecake. Bake in a preheated oven at 350 degrees for about 15 minutes. Check for doneness with a toothpick, stick a toothpick into one cake and pull out, it should be clean if it's done. The top of the cheesecakes should be a light brown. Let cool in a refrigerator and top with berries and serve chilled.

Mini Molten Chocolate Lava Cake with Raspberry Liquor

Rating: Moderate   Time: 45 minutes

Notes: 2-4 mini non-stick bundt cake pans or small ramekin / custard bowls can be used for this dessert.

Ingredients:

Your favorite commercial dark chocolate cake mix

32 oz semi sweet mini chocolate chips

1 tbsp sugar   Butter for greasing the cake pans

2 tbsp whole milk or half and half   Confectionary sugar

Optional: 1 tbsp of raspberry liquore
Directions:

Preheat the oven to the temperature recommended on the cake box. Follow the directions on the box for a cake but only use ½ of all the ingredients listed. Mix the ingredients with an electric mixer. Once combined add ½ cup of mini chocolate chips to the batter. Grease the bundt pans with butter. Pour the cake mix into the pans. The cakes will rise so do not fill the pans or cups to the top edge. Place the cake pans on a cookie sheet and bake on a middle-low rack in the preheated oven. Bake for 14 minutes and then check for doneness by sticking a toothpick into one of the cakes. If it comes out clean the cakes are done. Depending on the size of the cake pans that you're using the baking time may differ.

After the cakes have been removed from the oven to cool on a cooling rack, heat 3 to 4 inches of water in a sauce pan or double boiler. Once the water is simmering reduce the heat to medium low. Place a small metal bowl on the top of the pot and add the milk, the remaining chocolate chips and the sugar to the bowl, stirring with a wooden spoon. Once melted add the raspberry liquore (away from the burner) and stir. Turn off the heat when it's melted but leave the melted chocolate in the mixing bowl on top of the pot with the heated water, to keep the chocolate melted.

After cooling remove the cakes from the mini bundt cake pans to a plate. Pour the melted chocolate into the center of the bundt cakes to create a volcano effect with the chocolate as the lava in the center. Dust the cakes with confectionary sugar and serve.

Maple Flavored Fruit and Ice Cream

Rating: Easy   Time: 15-20 minutes
Ingredients:
Vanilla bean ice cream   ½ cup of roughly chopped walnuts
1 firm sweet apple or peach   1 cup of real maple syrup
Directions:

Peal and core the apple or peach and then cut it into wedges. In a medium sauce pan heat the syrup on medium heat until it simmers. Add the walnuts and the fruit and continue to heat the syrup for 2-3 minutes on medium low. Turn off the heat but leave the pan on the burner. Spoon the apples and walnuts over the ice cream and serve.

Dark Chocolate Mousse with Fresh Raspberries

Rating: Easy   Time: 30 minutes

Notes: We suggest that you make this dessert early in the day or the day before so that it has time to set up.

Ingredients:

16 oz dark chocolate, semi sweet   1 tbsp sugar

1 large egg   1 can real whipped cream

1 cup of heavy cream   8-10 fresh raspberries (Optional)

Directions:

Bring 3-4 inches of water to a low boil or simmer in a pot or double boiler, reduce the heat to medium low or low. Place a metal bowl that's larger than the pot on top of the pot of simmering water add the heavy cream and heat the cream until it's hot but not boiling. Break the chocolate into smaller pieces and add the chocolate and the sugar to the bowl of cream and melt the chocolate, stirring constantly with a wooden spoon. When the chocolate has completely melted remove it from the heat and let the bowl cool in a larger bowl of ice water.

Once the chocolate has cooled to room temperature separate the egg white from the egg yolk and pour egg white into a mixing bowl. Whip the egg white with an electric mixer until the egg whites stiffen and you get small peaks. Fold the egg white into the cooled chocolate, fully incorporate by stirring gently and then spoon the chocolate into 2 individual custard bowls or pudding dishes.

Cover the bowls with plastic wrap and let cool in the refrigerator for a couple of hours or longer until it's chilled. Squirt a little whipped cream on top and add a few raspberries and serve.

Banana's Sautéed in Brown Sugar

Rating: Easy   Time: 15 – 20 minutes

Ingredients:

2 ripe bananas, bite size pieces   Butter

2 tbsp brown sugar   1 can real whipped cream

Directions:

Heat 2-3 tbsp of butter in a small non-stick frying pan over medium heat. Be careful not to let the butter burn. Once the butter has melted add the bananas and brown sugar to the frying pan. Add more butter as it melts off. Heat the bananas and brown sugar until the sugar has dissolved and coated the bananas and the bananas are hot (about 2-3 minutes). Spoon the bananas onto 2 dessert plates and spray some whipped cream on top.

Chocolate, Cereal, Nuts & Fruit Dessert

Rating: Easy   Time: 5 Minutes

Ingredients:

3 cups Rice Chex ™ type cereal   ½ cup salted cashews

Confectionary sugar   ½ cup M&M ™ candies

½ cup dry roasted salted peanuts   ½ cup dried apricots

½ cup of another dried fruit, like pineapple or banana

Directions:

    Pour the cereal into a mixing bowl and sprinkle just enough confectionary sugar on top to coat the cereal (use the sugar somewhat sparingly). Then add all the other ingredients, mix and pour into a serving bowl and enjoy with a movie with your partner.

Mini Fresh Strawberry or Blueberry Pies

Rating: Moderate   Time: 1 hour

Ingredients:

12 oz fresh strawberries (or blueberries / raspberries)

1 package pre-made pie crust dough (both top & bottom)

1 tbsp mini chocolate chips or white chocolate morsels

2 or 3 oven safe custard bowls or ramekins

1 tbsp sugar   Non stick spray

1 can real whipped cream   Flour

Directions:

    Place the pie doughs (leaving them in their plastic wrapper) on the counter to bring them to room temperature.   Rinse and slice the strawberries and add to a mixing bowl with the sugar and stir gently. Cool in the refrigerator. Preheat the oven to 350 degrees. Dust a little flour on a large cutting board and lay one pie dough on top of the flour. Using a custard bowl or a ramekin place it upside down on the dough and cut a circle about 1 inch wider around than the circle created by the bowl with a small knife. This is the bottom dough. For the top dough cut a round that is equal to the circle created by placing the bowl upside down on the dough. Spray the bowl with non-stick spray and then place the bottom dough into the bowl and work it up the sides with your fingers so that it overflows the side of the bowl a little. Don't worry if you poke a hole in the dough.

Next, pour enough strawberries into the bowl to bring it to the top edge. Be sure to spoon in the juices as well. Then, place the top dough on top of the strawberries and with a fork, crimp the top dough to the bottom dough. Trim away any excess dough with a paring knife. Prick the dough 4-5 times with a knife and sprinkle some sugar on top. Repeat the process with the second bowl, and perhaps a third if you have enough ingredients left over. Place the bowls on a sheet pan and place on a middle rack and bake for about 20-25 minutes. The baking time may be a little more or less depending on the size of your bowls.

When the crust is a golden brown remove from the oven and let cool on a cooling rack. When you're ready to serve squirt with whipped cream and sprinkle a few chocolate chips on top.

Chocolate and Strawberry Parfait
Rating: Moderate   Time: 20 Minutes
Ingredients:
16 oz. strawberries, raspberries or blueberries
8 oz white chocolate chips, or dark
1 tbsp finely chopped pecans or walnuts
1 tbsp milk
1 can real whipped cream
Directions:
Wash and slice the strawberries, discarding the stems. Dry the berries on paper towels. Heat 2-3 inches of water in a double boiler pot to the point of a low simmer, reduce the heat to low. Place a metal bowl that is larger than the pot on top of the pot of simmering water and add the chocolate and milk. Stir the chocolate constantly until fully melted and turn off the heat, leaving the bowl on the pot to keep it warm. Add the nuts to the bowl and stir. In a tall wine or parfait glass place about 4-5 strawberry slices in the bottom of the glass and then drizzle the melted chocolate and nuts on top, about 1 tbsp. Add another layer of fruit and chocolate until the glass is full. Cool the glasses in the refrigerator for

20 minutes and remove and squirt with whipped cream and serve.

Chocolate and Brownie Parfait
Rating: Easy   Time: 10 Minutes
Ingredients:
2 brownies or cookies   1 can real whipped cream
16 oz mini chocolate chips   2 tbsp chopped walnuts
Vanilla chocolate swirl ice cream   2 tall wine glasses
Directions:

Buy 2-3 brownies or chocolate chip cookies from your grocery bakery. Break them into bite size pieces. To make the parfait, first add a scoop of ice cream to the glass. Then add a few chocolate chips and nuts and then add a couple brownie pieces. Repeat with another layer of ice cream, chocolate chips and nuts and then a brownie. At this point, depending on the height of your wine glasses you may want to top the last brownie with whipped cream and a sprinkling of nuts and chocolate chips on top of the whipped cream.

Peanut Butter and Chocolate Balls
Ratings: Challenging   Time: 20 Minutes
Ingredients:
4 oz dark semi sweet chocolate   Cocoa powder
4 oz peanut butter, chilled for 1 hr.   1 tbsp of finely chopped walnuts
1-2 tbsp milk   Wax paper
Directions:

In a double boiler heat 2 to 3 inches of water to a simmer. Place a large metal bowl on top of the pot and add 1 tbsp milk, sugar and the chocolate. Melt the chocolate slowly stirring regularly. If the melted chocolate is too thick, stir in a little more milk to make it easier to work with. The chocolate should be pourable. Once melted turn off the heat. Transfer the melted chocolate to a measuring cup with a spout.

Spread 2 – 3 tbsp of cocoa powder on a sheet of wax paper. Arrange a second sheet of wax paper on a dinner plate for the finished product. With a melon baller or teaspoon, scoop a ball of peanut butter onto the cocoa powder and roll into a ball with the palm of your hand (a teaspoon may come in handy to remove the peanut butter from the melon baller). Once the peanut butter is covered with cocoa powder it's easier to work with.   Arrange several of these peanut butter balls on wax paper (on a plate) and pour the hot chocolate on top and do not touch them until they harden. Sprinkle with some finely chopped walnuts if you like.

Once the plate is full of peanut butter and chocolate balls, transfer to the refrigerator to cool and harden, or freeze and eat frozen. Once they harden you can remove them from the wax paper.

Chocolate Covered Strawberries

Rating: Easy   Time: 15 - 20 minutes

Ingredients:

12-18 large strawberries washed, leave a portion of the stems on

1 lb. dark sweet or semi-sweet chocolate bar

1-2 tbsp milk, cream or half and half

Directions:

Heat 3 inches of water in a double boiler to a simmer and place a metal bowl (larger than the pot) on top of the pot. Break up the chocolate bar and place the pieces in the bowl along with the milk over the simmering water. Stir the chocolate as it melts with a wooden spoon. When the chocolate is all melted take the bowl off of the pot. While the chocolate is warm, dip the strawberries into the chocolate and cover the top portion of the berries, do not dip the stem end into the chocolate. Place each strawberry on a plate covered with wax paper, for cooling. Cool the plate in the refrigerator, cover the plate loosely with plastic wrap after the chocolate has hardened a bit. Serve chilled.

Breakfast Dishes

Poached Eggs Nested in Cheesy Grits

Rating: Moderate   Time: 30 minutes

Ingredients:

1 package of grits (any brand)   2 slices of bacon, cooked
1 cup shredded cheddar cheese   2 scallions chopped
2 tbsp shredded cheddar cheese   1 tsp white wine vinegar
2 large eggs   Salt and pepper

Directions:

Make about 2 cups of grits according to the directions on the box. When the grits are fully cooked stir 1 cup of cheddar cheese and scallions into the pot and remove from the stove and cover to keep warm. Season the grits with salt and pepper to taste. Dice the cooked bacon and stir into the grits.

Poach the two eggs as follows: In a medium skillet add about 1-1/2 inches of water and bring to a simmer on medium heat. Add the vinegar, which helps to keep the egg whites together when poaching. If you don't have cooking rings, simply crack 2 eggs into the simmering water (or use eggs rings). Poach the eggs as long as you like to. The longer you poach them the more fully cooked the yolks will be. Spoon the grits onto 2 plates and make a little hole in the middle to make a nest for the eggs. With a slotted spoon transfer one poached egg into one nest. Repeat for the second egg and the second nest. Season with salt and pepper, sprinkle the remaining cheddar cheese on top and serve.

Eggs in Toast

Rating: Moderate   Time: 20 minutes

Ingredients:

2 large fresh eggs
2 slices of bread (rye/whole grain)   Butter
Optional: hot sauce   Salt and pepper

Directions:

Toast the bread and then butter each slice thoroughly on both sides. Cut a round circle in both slices of toast about 2 inches in diameter. Heat a griddle or large non stick frying pan on medium heat. When it's warm add a couple of spoonfuls of butter to the pan being careful not to overheat the pan and burn the butter. Lay the slices of bread on the melted butter in the griddle (you may have to do each slice one at a time depending on the size of your pan). Crack one egg into a bowl or measuring cup. Then pour one egg into the hole in the toast. Repeat for the second egg. Cover the skillet with a large pot cover for a minute or two to cook the eggs to your liking. Season with salt and pepper and a couple of drops of hot sauce or ketchup, depending on what you like and serve.

Breakfast Egg and Cheddar Cheese Casserole

Rating: Easy   Time: 30 minutes

Ingredients:

4 large eggs

¼ cup half and half (or cream)

½ cup grated cheddar cheese

2 tbsp grated cheddar cheese

2 scallions chopped

¼ cup diced onion

½ cup red bell pepper chopped

1 tbsp chopped parsley

Salt and pepper

Non-stick cooking spray

Optional: ½ cup chopped cooked bacon/sausage

Directions:

Pre-heat oven to 375 degrees. Crack the eggs into a mixing bowl and add the half and half. Beat the eggs until the eggs are frothy. Season with salt and pepper. Spray the insides of two medium sized ramekins (or one small casserole dish) with cooking spray and add the vegetables, meat and ½ cup of cheese. Pour the eggs into the bowls and place on a sheet pan and bake uncovered for about 25 minutes or until the top is golden brown and the eggs are not runny. Open the oven and sprinkle 2 tbsp of cheddar cheese on top and close the oven, and wait for the cheese to start to melt. Remove the eggs from the oven, let cool a bit as they will be very hot.

Decadent Blueberry Pancakes

Rating: Moderate   Time: 30 minutes

Ingredients:

Pancake mix (your favorite)

4-6 oz frozen small blueberries

6 tbsp blueberry preserves

4 oz fresh blueberries

½ cup sliced almonds
100% pure maple syrup
Whipped butter

Non-stick cooking spray
Confectionary sugar

Directions:

    Heat the preserves in a bowl with a tsp of water in the microwave for 30 seconds. This will go fast so have the frozen blueberries and almonds next to the stove. Preheat oven to 250 degrees. Lightly grease a non-stick griddle or skillet with cooking spray and heat on medium. Mix the pancake batter according to the directions on the package for about 8 large pancakes. Stir the almonds right into the batter. Test to see if the griddle is hot enough by sprinkling a drop of water on it, the water should splatter or dance when it hits the griddle. When the griddle is ready, use a large mixing spoon to spoon the batter on the griddle to make a pancake about 6-7 inches wide. Then sprinkle a few frozen blueberries on the pancake. When one side of the pancake is golden brown flip and brown the other side, pressing down on the pancake with your spatula after flipping. You may need to turn down your heat to medium low if they brown too quickly, otherwise the center of the pancakes won't fully cook. Transfer each cooked pancake to an oven safe pan and keep them warm in the oven. Remember to spray your griddle a little after removing each pancake to prevent sticking. Once you have 8 pancakes you can start stacking.

    Heat 1 cup of maple syrup in a microwave oven for 30 seconds. To stack, place 1 pancake on a plate and with a spoon spread the warm blueberry preserves gently over the first pancake. Lay the second one on top and spread the butter. Then stack the third pancake and spread with blueberry preserves again. And then add the fourth and final pancake on top.

    Spread some butter on top, pour the warm maple syrup over the butter and then sprinkle the top with fresh blueberries. Dust the top with confectionary sugar or squirt on some whipped cream.

Killer French Toast

Rating: Easy

Time: 20 Minutes

Ingredients:
100% pure maple syrup
3 large eggs
Butter

Vegetable oil or cooking spray
1 tbsp ground cinnamon

One loaf of fresh and unsliced crusty bakery bread

Fresh fruit like: raspberries, blueberries, strawberries or chopped peaches

Directions:

Clean and taste the fruit. If the fruit is still a little tart and not sweet enough for your tastes, place the cut fruit in a bowl with a tbsp of sugar, stir and refrigerate.

Slice the bread extra thick, at least 1 inch thick. Slice 4 to 6 slices. In a large mixing bowl add the eggs and whisk well. Add 2 tbsp of maple syrup and the cinnamon and stir. Preheat the oven to 250 degrees. Heat a non-stick griddle or large frying pan on medium heat and spray with cooking spray. Dip the first slice of bread in the egg batter and make sure both sides are coated, letting any excess egg batter drip back into the bowl. Place the coated bread on the griddle when it's hot and repeat the process with a second slice. Watch the bread closely and as soon as the first side browns, flip it and brown the other side.

Remove the French toast to an oven safe dish and place in the oven to keep warm. Repeat the process until you've finish the batter. Serve the french toast with a pat of butter on top and several pieces of fruit and drizzle maple syrup over the top or a dusting of confectionary sugar.

Breakfast Burritos

Rating: Moderate   Time: 30 minutes

Ingredients:

4 large eggs   1 cup monterey jack cheese

2-3 tbsp half and half or whole milk   Non stick cooking spray

½ tsp ground cumin   ¼ tsp salt and pinch pepper

½ tsp chili powder   2 burrito size tortillas

2 tbsp salsa   Optional: sour cream

4 slices of bacon, diced and fried

2 tbsp jalapeno or bell pepper, chopped

Directions:

Make scrambled eggs: Crack the eggs into a mixing bowl and add the milk and whisk well. Add the cumin, chili powder and salt and pepper. Fry the eggs in a non-stick skillet that has been pre-oiled, stirring continuously with a spatula. Once the eggs are no longer runny remove the pan from the heat. Pre-heat the oven to 350 degrees.

Place the 2 tortillas on a plate and heat in the microwave oven for 30-45 seconds, to soften them. On a cookie sheet place a sheet of parchment paper and spray both sides of the paper, but if you don't have any parchment, simply spray the pan. Lay the first tortilla on pan and spoon on the cooked egg, chopped bacon, pepper and 1 tbsp of salsa. Then sprinkle a little cheese over the salsa. Roll the tortilla, leaving the ends open and the seam side down. Repeat with the second tortilla and bake for 5-10 minutes or until the cheese melts. Remove the burritos to a plate and spoon on a little sour cream.

INDEX

Lamb or veal shanks braised with pasta	60
Lasagna with meat sauce	70
Meatballs with sour cream over rice	71
Pasta salad with salami & provolone	71
Pork and rice Hawaiian style	68
Pork baby back ribs (easy)	64
Pork baby back ribs (moderate)	68
Pork chops grilled with peanut butter	69

Pork country ribs grilled & honey	66
Pork loin grilled & homemade BBQ	67
Pork tenderloin & balsamic vinegar	65
Steak and lobster tails	58
Steak grilled with mushrooms	56
Steak pocket pies	58
Veal cutlets sauté with mushrooms	64
Veal Osso Buco (easy)	63

Meatless Main Courses

Cappellini pasta with pesto sauce	73
Gnocchi with balsamic sauce	73
Linguini, onions and capers	74

Macaroni and cheese	74
Risotto with vegetables	75

Side Dishes

Apples baked with turnips	82
Baked beans Italian style	77
Brussels sprouts with maple syrup	77
Butternut squash roasted with honey	83
Carrots baked with horseradish	84
Cauliflower sautéed with onions	83
Coleslaw with horseradish	78
Corn on the cob grill roasted	85
Couscous	87
Green beans with tomatoes & bacon	78

Greens and beans	85
Greens sautéed with garlic olive oil	82
Kidney beans southwest style	86
Potato chips – broiled and healthy	79
Potatoes mashed with mushrooms	79
Red cabbage and apples with honey	87
Red potato salad	81
Spaghetti squash garlic sautéed	81
Spinach with creamy parmesan	80
Sweet potatoes roasted & creamy	86

Soups

Baked bean soup	89
Chunky chicken and pasta soup	92
Cream of asparagus soup	94
Creamy cauliflower soup	90
Creamy corn and ham soup	92
Greens and beans soup	95

Leak and potato creamy soup	88
Meatball soup	91
Potato and bacon cream soup	93
Roasted butternut squash soup	89
Salmon & cheese cream soup	94

Desserts

Baby chocolate cheesecakes	97
Banana's sautéed in brown sugar	99
Chocolate and brownie parfait	102
Chocolate and strawberry parfait	101
Chocolate covered strawberries	103
Chocolate lava cakes & raspberries	97

Chocolate mousse with raspberries	99
Chocolate, cereal, nuts and fruit mix	100
Maple flavored fruit & ice cream	98
Mini strawberry pies	100
Peanut butter and chocolate balls	102

Dry rub for meats – Here is a simple recipe for a dry rub if you don't have a favorite commercial brand: 2 tbsp paprika, 2 tsp salt and chili powder and 1 tsp each of the following: black pepper, ground thyme, onion powder, garlic powder, ground rosemary, ground cumin, ground sage and a ¼ tsp cayenne pepper. Feel free to leave out any ingredient that you don't like or add more cayenne for a spicy rub. Double the recipe for a larger batch.

19161093R00066

Made in the USA
Middletown, DE
09 April 2015